Cambridge Ele

Elements in Public Policy
edited by
M. Ramesh
National University of Singapore (NUS)
Michael Howlett
Simon Fraser University, British Columbia
Xun WU
Hong Kong University of Science and Technology
Judith Clifton
University of Cantabria
Eduardo Araral
National University of Singapore (NUS)

MULTIPLE STREAMS AND POLICY AMBIGUITY

Rob A. DeLeo
Bentley University

Reimut Zohlnhöfer
Heidelberg University

Nikolaos Zahariadis
Rhodes College

CAMBRIDGE
UNIVERSITY PRESS

Shaftesbury Road, Cambridge CB2 8EA, United Kingdom

One Liberty Plaza, 20th Floor, New York, NY 10006, USA

477 Williamstown Road, Port Melbourne, VIC 3207, Australia

314–321, 3rd Floor, Plot 3, Splendor Forum, Jasola District Centre,
New Delhi – 110025, India

103 Penang Road, #05–06/07, Visioncrest Commercial, Singapore 238467

Cambridge University Press is part of Cambridge University Press & Assessment,
a department of the University of Cambridge.

We share the University's mission to contribute to society through the pursuit of
education, learning and research at the highest international levels of excellence.

www.cambridge.org
Information on this title: www.cambridge.org/9781009494502

DOI: 10.1017/9781009397926

© Rob A. DeLeo, Reimut Zohlnhöfer, and Nikolaos Zahariadis 2024

This publication is in copyright. Subject to statutory exception and to the provisions
of relevant collective licensing agreements, no reproduction of any part may take
place without the written permission of Cambridge University Press & Assessment.

When citing this work, please include a reference to the DOI 10.1017/9781009397926

First published 2024

A catalogue record for this publication is available from the British Library.

ISBN 978-1-009-49450-2 Hardback
ISBN 978-1-009-39791-9 Paperback
ISSN 2398-4058 (online)
ISSN 2514-3565 (print)

Cambridge University Press & Assessment has no responsibility for the persistence
or accuracy of URLs for external or third-party internet websites referred to in this
publication and does not guarantee that any content on such websites is, or will
remain, accurate or appropriate.

Multiple Streams and Policy Ambiguity

Elements in Public Policy

DOI: 10.1017/9781009397926
First published online: February 2024

Rob A. DeLeo
Bentley University

Reimut Zohlnhöfer
Heidelberg University

Nikolaos Zahariadis
Rhodes College

Author for correspondence: Rob A. DeLeo, rdeleo@bentley.edu

Abstract: The last decade has seen a proliferation of research bolstering the theoretical and methodological rigor of the Multiple Streams Framework (MSF), one of the most prolific theories of agenda-setting and policy change. This Element sets out to address some of the most prominent criticisms of the theory, including the lack of empirical research and the inconsistent operationalization of key concepts, by developing the first comprehensive guide for conducting MSF research. It begins by introducing the MSF, including key theoretical constructs and hypotheses. It then presents the most important theoretical extensions of the framework and articulates a series of best practices for operationalizing, measuring, and analyzing MSF concepts. It closes by exploring existing gaps in MSF research and articulating fruitful areas of future research.

Keywords: multiple streams framework, agenda-setting, policy change, policy entrepreneurship, policy windows

© Rob A. DeLeo, Reimut Zohlnhöfer, and Nikolaos Zahariadis 2024

ISBNs: 9781009494502 (HB), 9781009397919 (PB), 9781009397926 (OC)
ISSNs: 2398-4058 (online), 2514-3565 (print)

Contents

1 Current Trends in Multiple Streams Research

Originally developed by John Kingdon in his 1984 book *Agendas, Alternatives, and Public Policies*, the Multiple Streams Framework (MSF) is designed to explain policymaking under conditions of ambiguity or situations when there is more than one way of thinking about the same problem. To accomplish this task, Kingdon uses a fairly straightforward metaphor characterizing the policy process as encompassing three distinct streams of activity – a problem, policy, and politics stream. On occasion, the streams present a policy window, which he describes as an often fleeting opportunity to merge or couple the three streams and, in turn, induce agenda-setting. The theory further argues that coupling is facilitated by *policy entrepreneurs*, a term describing individuals who invest considerable time, energy, and resources in pursuit of agenda change (Kingdon 2003: 179).

The MSF's fairly accessible depiction of the policy process has made it one of the most widely applied frameworks within the policy sciences. A simple Google Scholar search yields over 30,000 citations of Kingdon's book alone and recent meta-reviews have unearthed hundreds of peer-reviewed publications applying the framework (Jones et al. 2016; Rawat and Morris 2016; see also Béland and Howlett 2016). However, despite the MSF's popularity, applications of the theory have been criticized for lacking rigor and failing to consistently define, operationalize, and measure key concepts (Béland and Howlett 2016; Cairney and Jones 2016; Jones et al. 2016). An international network of scholars has responded to these critiques by developing a research agenda for the MSF that is founded in shared hypotheses (Herweg, Zahariadis, and Zohlnhöfer 2023; Zohlnhöfer, Herweg, and Zahariadis 2022), a commitment to systematically testing key research questions (e.g., DeLeo and Duarte 2022; Dolan 2021), and a desire to test the theory's explanatory power in a variety of geographic and policymaking contexts (e.g., Goyal 2022; van den Dool 2023b; Herweg, Zahariadis, and Zohlnhöfer 2022).

A number of recent studies have made strides in articulating best practices for applying the MSF; however, much of this work remains diffuse and spread out across various edited volumes (Herweg, Zahariadis, and Zohlnhöfer 2023; Zohlnhöfer, Herweg, and Zahariadis 2022) and journal articles (Hoefer 2022; Jones et al. 2016). This level of fragmentation makes it challenging to develop a coherent research agenda since it heightens the risk of scholars talking past one another and defaulting to haphazard applications of core theoretical concepts. Complicating matters further, Kingdon's robust use of metaphors raises the specter of varying and at times incongruent conceptualizations of core concepts. Indeed, in one of the most comprehensive assessments of the theory to date, Jones et al. (2016: 30) observed that "While MSA analysts use the same vocabulary they do not all share the same definition of concepts," which has, in turn, stunted robust theoretical development.

The following Element helps remedy these shortcomings by combining and elaborating on these important works in a single, authoritative text. In doing so, it seeks to promote greater ease of application by providing, for lack of a better term, a "one stop shop" that emerging and seasoned MSF scholars can turn to when applying the theory. In the pages that follow, we will walk the reader through the various steps involved in developing an MSF study, describing best practices, highlighting existing gaps in the literature, and, where possible, spotlighting exemplar studies.

Our Element will proceed as follows. The remainder of this section will provide a very brief introduction to the MSF, including key assumptions and the various elements. (Note that all of these items will be explored in greater detail in coming sections.) It then presents various indicators of MSF's growth over the last decade plus, including the number of articles applying the framework, the framework's application in new and novel contexts, the various methodologies used to study the MSF, and other useful metrics contextualizing the MSF's evolution.

Section 2 will zero-in on the three streams and provide a detailed assessment of the key elements associated with each stream (indicators, focusing events, the national mood, etc.), the role of policy entrepreneurs in determining the trajectory of agenda-setting, and the various types of policy windows. This section will close by outlining the hypotheses developed to test these concepts, including the various studies that have attempted to test them.

Having provided an introduction to the theory, Section 3 will familiarize readers with the various extensions that have been suggested in the last decade to make the framework applicable to various stages of the policy cycle in addition to agenda-setting for which it was originally developed (e.g., decision-making, policy implementation and policy termination). Section 3 will also consider whether MSF can be used to explain the scale and scope of policy change.

Section 4 will continue to push on the theme of MSF extensions; however, instead of focusing on the different stages of the policy process it will focus on recent attempts to apply the MSF to new governing contexts. It begins by exploring the research applying MSF to presidential systems outside the United States (e.g., Latin America) before examining applications in parliamentary and authoritarian contexts. Section 4 will also assess recent attempts to apply the framework in international and supranational organizations, most importantly the European Union (EU). It closes by describing some of the opportunities and challenges associated with applying MSF to multilevel governing contexts.

Section 5 articulates best practices for conducting an MSF study. It will begin by exploring the various types of qualitative and quantitative data used to measure key elements in the problem, policy, and political streams; policy windows; policy entrepreneurship; and other theoretical constructs. It will also examine the trade-offs associated with conducting qualitative, quantitative, or mixed-method MSF studies. It will include a series of examples featuring exemplar studies to help illustrate best practices.

The Element will close in Section 6 by briefly summarizing key findings from each of the previous sections, paying particularly close attention to future research directions.

1.1 A Brief Primer on the MSF

The following section very briefly introduces the MSF. (The following section provides a much more granular assessment of the theory and its structural elements.) MSF draws its inspiration from Cohen, March, and Olsen's (1972) garbage can model of organizational choice. Cohen, March, and Olsen characterize organizations as "organized anarchies," marked by six overarching features: (1) ambiguity; (2) time constraints; (3) problematic preferences; (4) unclear technology; (5) fluid participation; and (6) stream independence.

It is MSF's sixth assumption that tends to receive the most scholarly attention. Figure 1 provides an overview of the theory's structural elements. Broadly, MSF assumes three distinct streams of policy activity. The *problem stream* denotes the various issues and items vying for policymaker attention. The *policy stream* describes the various ideas and, in some cases, policy solutions developed by actors operating within and outside government. The *political stream* describes the constellation of political factors influencing issue attention and agenda-setting.

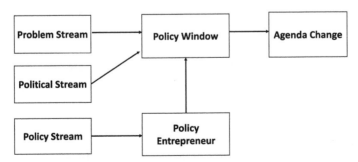

Figure 1 Diagram of the multiple streams framework.
Adapted from Zahariadis (2003).

Broadly, MSF assumes the three streams need to be coupled in order for agenda-setting to occur. Coupling is made possible by the opening of a "policy window." MSF further argues that policy entrepreneurs, or individuals who invest considerable time, energy, and resources to promote policy change, help facilitate coupling by demonstrating a connection between their preferred solution and a problem circulating the problem stream. With this basic introduction of the theory in mind, we now turn our attention to the current state of MSF research.

1.2 MSF Applications across Time

A 2016 meta-review by Jones et al. provides one of the most comprehensive assessments of MSF's development across time to date. The article assessed over 300 peer-reviewed journal articles testing MSF concepts between the years 2000 and 2013. Jones et al. provide a proverbial treasure trove of descriptive statistics measuring everything from the geographic areas studied by MSF researchers to the policy domains investigated in each article, author affiliations to research methodologies, level of governance to key findings regarding specific aspects of the theory (e.g., the problem stream, policy entrepreneurship, policy windows). By highlighting existing gaps within the extant research as well as strategies for ensuring the theory's continued growth and development, this paper has served as a springboard for contemporary MSF research.

Almost ten years have passed since Jones et al.'s (2016) paper was first published, suggesting the need to revisit the state of MSF publications. To this end, the following section provides a much needed update to the 2016 meta-review by examining MSF applications over the course of the following nine years. We specifically focus on what the 2016 meta-review called "descriptors of applications" or data documenting the volume and nature of MSF applications between 2014 and 2022. This section aims to provide, for lack of a better term, a "four thousand foot view" of MSF's growth in the wake of the 2016 meta-review.

To this end, we more or less replicate the data collection strategy used by Jones et al. (2016). We specifically relied on the Web of Science data to develop a comprehensive list of all articles citing MSF between 2014 and 2022. We utilize the same search criteria applied by Jones et al.: (1) citations of Kingdon's *Agendas, Alternatives, and Public Policies*;[1] and (2) citations of the various MSF sections written for the 1999, 2007, 2014, and 2018 versions of *Theories of the Policy Process*.[2] Our analysis only included peer-reviewed journals available in

---

[1] Like Jones et al. (2016) we use all variant publication years of *Agendas, Alternatives and Public Policies*, most notably 1984, 1995, 1996, 1997, 2002, 2003, 2005, 2006, 2010, and 2011.

[2] Note that the 2018 version of the *Theories of the Policy Process* was not available when "A River Runs through It" was published.

English. This search yielded a total of 3,459 articles, nearly double the number unearthed by the 2016 meta-review.

In order to develop a more manageable corpus of articles, we asked two coders to determine whether each was applying the MSF or if it simply made a passing reference to the theory without actively engaging core concepts. Specifically, in order to be considered an application of the MSF, the author(s) need to explicitly state within their abstract that their article applies/tests/ examines MSF. Articles that failed to do this were excluded from our study. This initial review allowed us to narrow our list of articles to n=334.

Of these articles, 78% (261 articles) were further classified as empirical applications of the MSF, meaning they sought to apply or at least leverage the theory to explain a case/topical area of interest. The remaining 22% (73 articles) were classified as empirical synthetic, meaning they apply MSF alongside other theories of the policy process. Note that a handful of studies were excluded from our analysis because they did not use any stated methodology, but were purely theory building exercises, thought pieces, or reviews.

Having described our data collection protocol, the following section will explore various indicators of growth and application over the course of the last nine years. Because subsequent sections provide a detailed account of recent conceptual advances, including theoretical extensions, novel methodological approaches, and hypothesis testing and development, this analysis focuses primarily on describing the breadth and scope of MSF applications across time. Unlike Jones et al. (2016), we do not, for example, document how many studies examined the various elements of the problem stream (e.g., indicators, focusing events, feedback) or the number of studies referencing policy windows. These topics are covered in greater detail later in the Element. Instead, we focus our attention on the (1) number of applications published by year; (2) publication outlets and author affiliation; (3) policy domains; (4) geographic focus and type of regime (democracy vs. autocracy); (5) level of governance; and (6) methodology.

1.2.1 MSF Publications per Year

Jones et al. (2016) report a marked uptick in annual MSF publications between 2000 (11 articles) and 2013 (41 articles). Figure 2 suggests this trend has continued over the last nine years, which has seen the number of MSF publication increase from nineteen articles in 2014 to a whopping fifty-nine articles in 2022. The lowest number of publications per year never dipped below eighteen (2015), which is nearly two times higher than the lowest number reported by Jones et al. The highest number of publications (59 articles in 2022) is noticeably larger than the previous high of 45 articles

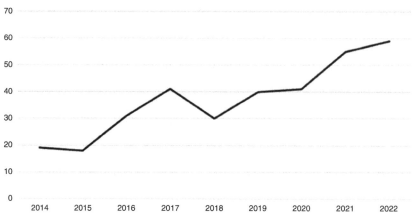

Figure 2 MSF refereed publications by year.

Years published: 2014 (19), 2015 (18), 2016 (31), 2017 (41), 2018 (30), 2019 (40), 2020 (41), 2021 (55), 2022 (59)

recorded in 2011 (Figure 2). Taken together, this data suggests MSF has grown over the last nine years and remains on an upward trajectory.

1.2.2 Publication Outlets and Author Affiliation

MSF continues to find its way into a fairly diverse array of publication outlets. Whereas Jones et al. (2016) note that MSF appeared in 165 different peer-reviewed journals between 2000 and 2013, our analysis identified MSF applications in 201 different peer-reviewed journals, further proof of the theory's proliferation across time. Not surprisingly, MSF articles continue to be widely published in journals that identify as generalist public administration and public policy outlets (e.g., *Policy Sciences, Policy Studies Journal, Public Administration*) as well as journals more narrowly focused on specific policy areas like health (*Global Public Health, Health Policy and Planning, Health Systems & Reform*), energy and the environment (*Energy Policy, Environmental Planning C*), education (*Education Policy, Education Research for Policy and Practice*), and even sports (*Sport, Education and Society; International Journal of Sport Policy and Politics*). Journals publishing five or more MSF articles include *Journal of Comparative Policy Analysis* (10), *Policy Studies Journal* (9), *Policy Sciences* (9), *International Journal of Sports Policy and Politics* (6), *Health Research Policy and Systems* (6), *Energy Research & Social Science* (6), *Food Policy* (5), *Environmental Politics* (5), and *Energy Policy* (5). Curiously, unlike Jones et al., we find scant evidence of widespread applications in more mainstream political science journals.

Author affiliation information was made available through Web of Science. More authors are affiliated with European institutions than any other region in the world (n=366). The lion's share of these authors is from institutions in the United Kingdom (122) or Germany (61), although the Netherlands (35), Italy (16), Switzerland (14), Belgium (13), Norway (13), Austria (12), France (10), and Spain (10) are also fairly well represented. It is notable that the number of authors affiliated with institutions in the United Kingdom more than doubled and, in the case of Germany, more than tripled since Jones et al.'s (2016) publication. This said, the overwhelming majority of MSF articles were published by authors affiliated with institutions in the United States (197) (Figure 3).

We observe a marked uptick in author affiliations outside of North America and Europe. For example, the number of authors affiliated with institutions located in Asia increased from 20 individuals at the time of Jones et al.'s study to 116 individuals in our study. The number of authors affiliated with institutions located in Africa jumped from nine individuals to fifty-four individuals. Similarly, the number of authors affiliated within institutions located in Oceania increased from twenty-one to seventy-eight individuals. Perhaps most impressive, whereas Jones et al. (2016) do not report a single MSF publication by authors affiliated with South American institutions, we find more than forty articles including at least one author affiliated with institutions located in South America (Figure 3). Taken together, this data suggests the theory has made significant gains in attracting engagement from scholars across the globe.[3]

1.2.3 Policy Domain

Consistent with Jones et al. (2016), we coded for a total of twenty-two discreet policy domain categories: Health, Environment, Governance, Education, Welfare, Agriculture, Arts, Defense, Diversity, Economics, Emergency Services, Energy, Firearms, Foreign Relations, Justice, Labor, Nonprofit, Planning/Development, Real Estate, Religion, Technology, and Transportation. Three articles were coded as "not applicable" because they either failed to specify a domain or focused on a topical area that is not represented by our existing codebook (e.g., women's studies).

Like Jones et al. (2016), we find that health, 27% (e.g., Bandelow et al. 2017); governance, 25% (e.g., Engl and Evrard 2020); and the environment, 13% (e.g., Conceição et al. 2015) are by far the most popular domains explored by MSF studies. We find that education, 6% (e.g., Cummings Strunk, and De Voto. 2023);

---

[3] Recall too that our study, like Jones et al. (2016), only considers peer-review articles written in English. These numbers would likely be much higher had we included articles written in other languages.

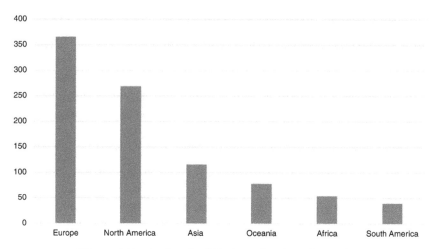

Figure 3 Institutional affiliation of authors by region

Institutional affiliation of author by region. A number of authors had multiple affiliations. **Europe:** United Kingdom **(122)**, Germany **(61)**, Netherlands **(35)**, Italy **(16)**, Switzerland **(14)**, Belgium **(13)**, Norway **(13)**, Austria **(12)**, France **(10)**, Spain **(10)**, Denmark **(9)**, Ireland **(9)**, Finland **(8)**, Portugal **(8)**, Czech Republic **(7)**, Russia **(5)**, Sweden **(5)**, Hungary **(4)**, Croatia **(2)**, Luxembourg **(2)**, Romania **(1)**; **North America:** United States **(197)**, Canada **(68)**, Mexico **(4)**; **Asia:** Iran **(31)**, Japan **(18)**, Malaysia **(9)**, South Korea **(7)**, Lebanon **(6)**, Singapore **(6)**, India **(5)**, Taiwan **(5)**, Kuwait **(3)**, Turkey **(3)**, Israel **(2)**, Vietnam **(2)**, Indonesia **(1)**, Philippines **(1)**, Saudi Arabia **(1)**; **Oceania:** Australia **(73)**, New Zealand (5); **Africa:** South Africa (18); Ghana (7); Guinea (7); Cameroon (6), Uganda (5), Burkina Faso (2), Chad (2), Namibia (2), Zambia (2), Zimbabwe (2), Egypt **(1)**; **South America:** Brazil (25), Barbados (7), Chile (2), Paraguay (2), Argentina (2)

economics, 5% (e.g., Spognardi 2020); and energy, 5% (e.g., Kagan 2019) are also popular domains. The remaining 19% of MSF papers (our "other" category) encompass a fairly eclectic mix of policy areas ranging from agriculture (e.g., Faling and Biesbroek 2019) to emergency services (e.g., Eckersley and Lakoma 2021) (Figure 4).

1.2.4 Geographic Area and Regime Studied

In addition to measuring the institutional affiliation of authors publishing MSF studies, we also collected data on the country or, in a number of cases, countries studied in each article. In total, we identified sixty-six different countries, suggesting significant geographic variation within the MSF literature. Figure 5 reports the results of our analysis, grouping the various countries in the same six regions used by Jones et al. (2016): Europe, North America, Asia, Oceania, South America, and Africa.

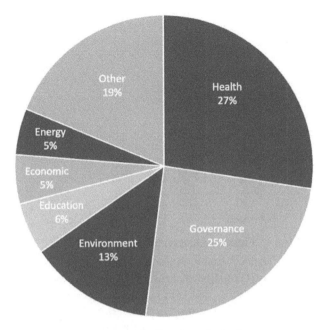

Figure 4 Policy domain foci

Some articles fell into more than one policy domain, but none fell into more than three. **Health** (94); **Governance** (84); **Environment** (46); **Education** (19); **Economic** (18). **Energy** (17); **Other**: Planning (14); Technology (12); Justice (7); Welfare (6); Labor (4); Defense (3); Foreign Relations (2); Agriculture (1); Diversity (1); Nonprofit (1)

The overwhelming majority of studied countries are in either Europe (n=120) (e.g., Kristiansen and Houlihan 2015; Carter and Childs 2017; Derwort, Jager, and Newig 2021) or North America (n=80) (e.g., Anderson and Maclean 2015; Carriedo, Lock, and Hawkins 2020; Tunstall et al. 2015), which echoes Jones et al.'s (2016) findings. The number of MSF articles published on Asian countries (n=52) (e.g., van den Dool 2023a; Tanaka et al. 2020) remains quite strong. Unfortunately, applications to South America (n=38) (e.g., Araújo and Dinara Leslye Macedo e Silva Calazans 2020; Bossert and Dintrans 2020; Ryan and Micozzi 2021), Oceania (n=27) (e.g., Harris and McCue 2023; Smith and Cumming 2017; Schührer 2018), and Africa (n=20) (e.g., Ssengooba et al. 2021; Tembo and Lim 2022; Hassanin 2021) are modest in comparison to other regions, suggesting these regions may provide a fruitful context for testing the theory. Not reported in Figure 5 are the multitude of studies (n=38) applying MSF to international and regional governing organizations, such as the European Union (e.g., Kaunert and Léonard 2019), United Nations (e.g., Jakobsson 2021), and the International Olympic Committee (e.g., Pack and Hedlund 2020).

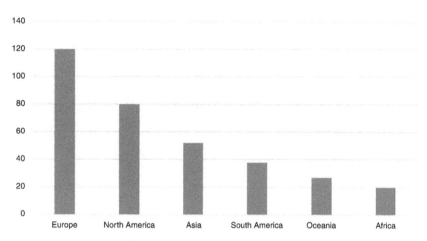

Figure 5 Geographic area studied.

Location of study by region. A number of articles studied multiple areas. Europe: United Kingdom (42), Germany (11), Ireland (9), France (8), Russia (6), Norway (6), Austria (6), Portugal (4), Italy (4), Sweden (3), Denmark (3), Belgium (2), Croatia (2), Czech Republic (2), Finland (2), Greece (2), Netherlands (2), Spain (2), Switzerland (2), Romania (1), Scotland (1); **North America**: United States (62), Canada (16), Mexico (2); **Asia**: China (10), India (8), Iran (7), Japan (5), Turkey (4), Malaysia (3), South Korea (2), Lebanon (2), Hong Kong (2), Indonesia (1), Kuwait (1), Maldives (1), Mauritius (1), Myanmar (1), the Philippines (1), Singapore (1), Taiwan (1), Vietnam (1); **South America**: Chile (14), Brazil (13), Costa Rica (2), Ecuador (2), Peru (2), Argentina (1), Barbados (1), Belize (1), Paraguay (1), Uruguay (1); **Oceania**: Australia (25), New Zealand (2); **Africa**: Uganda (3), South Africa (3), Egypt (2), Ghana (2), Kenya (2), Cameroon (1), Chad (1), Guinea (1), Namibia (1), Tanzania (1), Tunisia (1), Zambia (1)

Even with these regional imbalances, the geographic diversity of MSF studies, particularly when disaggregated to the country-level, is impressive. MSF studies have been applied to a fairly wide array of countries from Iran (e.g., Moghadam Raeissi, and Jafari-Sirizi 2019) to Tanzania (e.g., Fischer and Strandberg-Larsen 2016) and from Romania (e.g., Wang et al. 2021) to Cameroon (e.g., Sieleunou et al. 2017). The variety of geographic applications suggests MSF remains a theory that travels well and can be used to explain a variety of governing contexts outside of the United States.

To further differentiate between the various countries studied, we assessed each country's Global Freedom Score. Global Freedom Scores rate individuals' access to political rights and civil liberties. This data is available on the Freedom House website.[4] As shown in Figure 6, 59% (thirty-nine of the sixty-six countries) of

---

[4] Freedom House scores can be accessed here: https://freedomhouse.org/countries/freedom-world/scores.

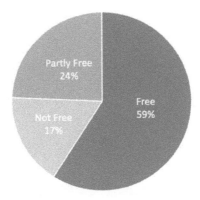

Figure 6 Global Freedom Scores of countries studied in MSF articles.

the countries studied were classified as "free," 24% (n=16) were classified as "partly free" (n=11), and 17% were classified as "not free." These findings provide further evidence of the considerable variety of national policymaking contexts within which MSF is studied.

1.2.5 Governance Level

In addition to coding for the geographic focus of each article, we also coded for the level of government studied. Again, consistent with Jones et al. (2016), we coded for five levels of government: local, state, regional, national, and international/transnational. Not surprisingly, a number of studies explored multiple levels of government. We identified a total of 337 different governance codes across out 334 articles, a testament to the fact that a few studies explored multiple levels.[5]

The overwhelming majority of articles (67%) were coded as national government (e.g., Akgul, Akbas, and Kule 2019), while 15% were coded as transnational/international (e.g., Jakobsson 2021), 10% as state (e.g., Collins 2017), 7% as local (e.g., O'Neill, Kapoor, and McLaren 2019) and only 1% as regional (e.g., Johnstone 2018) (Figure 7). Jones et al. (2016) also found a preference for national studies. Our findings suggest more work is needed to expand MSF application in subnational contexts, which have played an increasingly important role in shaping policy within federal systems.

---

[5] Note that our analysis differs slightly from Jones et al. (2016) in that we instructed coders to consider the primary focus of each article. Put differently, which level of government is most prominent in each article? This approach results in far fewer instances of articles being coded as having multiple-levels in comparison to Jones et al.

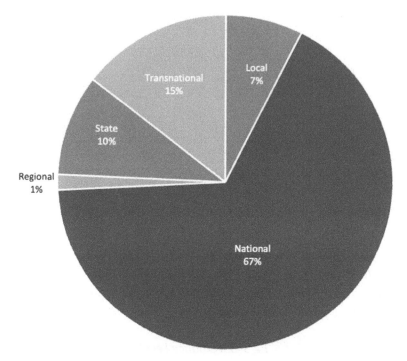

Figure 7 Level of governance studied.

1.2.6 Methodology

Coders were instructed to consider three different areas when coding for methodology: quantitative, qualitative, and mixed. Qualitative studies were defined as any study that does not use numerical data beyond descriptive statistics. The overwhelming majority of the studies we coded were qualitative (90%, n=280) (e.g., van den Dool 2023b; Koebele 2021; O'Neill, Kapoor, and McLaren 2019) (Figure 8). Jones et al. (2016) similarly found that the vast majority of the studies in their sample (88%) were qualitative.

Far fewer articles employed either a mixed methods or quantitative approach. Specifically, twenty articles (7%) were coded as mixed methods (e.g., DeLeo and Duarte 2022), while only ten articles (3%) were coded as quantitative (e.g., Fowler 2022) (Figure 8). Jones et al. (2016) suggest these disparities may be attributable to difficulties operationalizing MSF constructs in ways that can be readily measured quantitatively (see Engler and Herweg 2019). Our data suggest operationalization remains a vexing issue for the theory. To this end, subsequent sections will explore potential paths forward for researchers hoping to employ quantitative techniques.

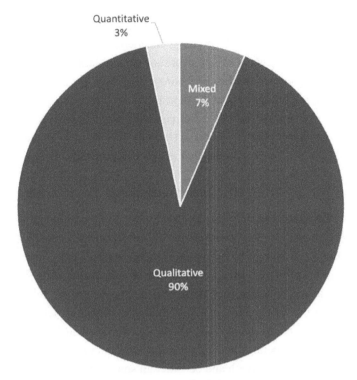

Figure 8 Methodology.

2 The Main Model: Assumptions, Main Elements, and Key Hypotheses

Having explored trends in MSF research across time, we now turn our attention to a detailed introduction to the core assumptions and concepts comprising the MSF, in turn providing intellectual scaffolding for accompanying sections. We first introduce MSF's six assumptions before walking through the theory's structural elements, namely the problem, politics, and policy streams; policy entrepreneurship; and policy windows. We close by listing the various hypotheses associated with the MSF as well as a number of studies that either explicitly or implicitly inform these hypotheses.

2.1 Assumptions

As noted in the previous section, MSF borrows from Cohen, March, and Olsen's (1972) garbage can model of organizational choice to derive six key assumptions. The following section takes a closer look at these six assumptions before unpacking the framework's various structural features.

2.1.1 Ambiguity

MSF is designed to explain policymaking under conditions of ambiguity. Not to be confused with uncertainty, which denotes a general lack of understanding or information, ambiguity describes situations where there are multiple and often competing ways of thinking about the same problem. In this respect, the presence of ambiguity means policy debates are often settled not through facts or even data, but through problem definition, a concept broadly describing the process through which competing interests assign meaning to social problems.

2.1.2 Time Constraints

Whereas individuals can only attend effectively to one or a handful issues at a time, organizations, like government, can process many issues simultaneously. This is, in large part, testament to the division of labor, which allows different groups to work through more or less discreet items at the same time. Although a division of labor is obviously advantageous since it helps to facilitate greater organization efficiency, it also creates situations where there are multiple and competing items vying for policymaker attention. As a result, policymakers often operate under extreme time constraints, which, in turn, limit their ability to carefully weigh and consider all solutions to a given problem.

2.1.3 Problematic Preferences

Policymaker preferences are said to be malleable. Specifically, their policy preferences evolve and change across time, often in response to interactions with organized interests, constituents, experts, fellow policymakers, and other actors involved in the policy process. Thus, MSF assumes that policymakers can adjust their policy preferences across time and in response to different interpersonal and environmental (e.g., changing information) factors. Note, however, that only policymakers' policy preferences are assumed to be problematic. These actors do have rather clear preferences regarding the outcome of the next election or the composition of the next government. Moreover, the assumption of problematic preferences does not exclude the possibility that policymakers have certain political leanings (e.g., left-right or pro/against government intervention).

2.1.4 Unclear Technology

The term "technology," at least within the context of the MSF, refers to the processes that transform inputs (e.g., problems and demands) into outputs (e.g., solutions). Technology lacks clarity, meaning government jobs and responsibilities are often poorly articulated and undefined. Jurisdictional boundaries are often overlapping and unclear, thereby heightening the possibility of conflict and turf battles between different agencies and organizations.

2.1.5 Fluid Participation

Policymaking institutions are dynamic: elections change the composition of legislature; bureaucrats are hired, fired, and retire; even judges are subject to change. MSF thus assumes the composition of decision-making bodies is fluid and changes across time. This reshuffling of key positions within government, in turn, creates new pathways for change since each participant brings with them a new set of priorities and perspectives.

2.1.6 Stream Independence

Last but certainly not least, MSF assumes three "more or less" independent streams flow through the policymaking system: a problem stream, a policy stream, and a political stream. Stream independence implies two things. First, streams develop mostly independent of one another: solutions are developed regardless of what is happening in the politics stream, but also – much more importantly – of what problems are currently on the agenda. Similarly, problems occur independently of the current government or the national mood and vice versa. Of course, stream independence is not considered absolute as there are clearly instances when at least two streams interact outside policy windows (where the streams come together to get coupled according to MSF thinking). Nonetheless, stream independence is considered a helpful analytical device. Second (but related), each stream follows its own rules and dynamic that are quite distinct from those of the other streams, as we will demonstrate in Sections 2.2.1–2.2.3.

2.2 Main Elements: Streams, Windows, Coupling, and the Policy Entrepreneur

As indicated previously, MSF conceptualizes the policy process as consisting of three more or less discreet streams of activity: problem, policy, and political streams. The theory argues that the three streams need to be "coupled" or brought together for agenda-setting to occur and that coupling is made possible by the opening of a "policy window." The theory further emphasizes the critical importance of policy entrepreneurs, who facilitate coupling by highlighting linkages across the three streams. The accompanying section explores each of these elements in greater detail.

2.2.1 Problem Stream

The problem stream consists of all the issues or problems competing for public and policymaker attention. More specifically, the problem stream spotlights various mechanisms through which issues generate attention: indicators, focusing events, and feedback. Kingdon describes *indicators* as "more or less" objective or systematic numerical measures and metrics of a problem. Examples include highway deaths, disease rates, consumer prices, and scores of others. Most indicators are the byproduct of routine monitoring by government and nongovernmental agencies. However, Kingdon is careful to note that certain types of studies and reports aggregating and interpreting these data can help bring new indicators to light. Indicators derive their agenda-setting power from the fact that they are countable, which, for better or worse, can create the perception that these numbers are more objective representations of a problem (Kingdon 2003), although other research suggests certain domains have stronger indicator cultures than others (Bell et al. 2011; Turnhout, Hisschemöller, and Eijsackers 2007).

When and under what conditions do indicators facilitate an uptick in policymaker attention? Kingdon (2003: 92) notes that "Policy makers consider a change in an indicator to be a change in the state of a system: this they define as a problem." Still, it is less clear just how much an indicator needs to change or deteriorate in order to raise a particular domain's prominence within the problem stream. DeLeo (2018) suggests that rapid indicator accumulation, which refers to situations in which indicators amass quickly and over a short period of time, tends to garner significant media and policymaker attention, in part because these changes are seemingly too great to ignore. However, rapid indicator accumulation is not automatically a recipe for coupling, since the other streams may need time to ripen and catch up to the sudden changes in a problem's condition. To this end, DeLeo shows a more gradual, but persistent, change in indicators is, at least in some cases, a more fruitful pathway to agenda-setting and policy change since it allows the other streams to fully gestate.

Of course, whether an indicator changes rapidly or gradually matters little if organized interests shield policymaker attention from these changes in a problem's condition. In their study of opioid policymaking, DeLeo and Duarte (2022) show indicator politicization, which describes the extent to which indicator change is perceived as a threat – economic, political, or otherwise – to actors operating in the political stream, is inversely related to issue attention. More specifically, highly politicized indicators tend to blunt policymaker attention to changes within the problem stream regardless of the rate of indicator change, thus providing somewhat countervailing evidence to the argument that indicator deterioration equates to agenda change.

In fairness, Kingdon (2003) himself suggests that, in some cases, indicator change alone is not a sufficient catalyst for agenda change. Instead, a problem may "need a little push to get the attention of people in and around government" (p. 94). That push can come in the form of a *focusing event*. Focusing events can come in various forms and flavors, ranging from a large-scale disaster that seemingly bowls over other agenda items (see Birkland 1997) to a personal experience of a policymaker (see Craig et al. 2010) to the emergence of a powerful symbol that comes to represent a larger social issue (see Brunner 2008).

Subsequent work has sought to refine Kingdon's conceptualization of focusing events to make it more amendable to systematic assessment. Birkland (1997) defines potential focusing events as events that are sudden, rare, reveal actual or potential harms, are known to the public and policymakers virtually simultaneously, and are concentrated on a community of interest (Birkland 1997; see also O'Donovan 2017; Craig et al. 2010). It is critical to underscore that an event's focal power is by no means predetermined. Many disasters fail to trigger any response from government, let alone help to facilitate the opening of a policy window. Those events that do induce change often come to symbolize examples of government failure in addition to revealing significant harms (Birkland 1997).

The third and final element of the problem stream, *feedback*, refers to information about the current administration of government programs (Kingdon 2003). Feedback, which, at least in the context of MSF, is one of the more understudied elements of the problem stream, can range from systematic and routinized evaluations to informal complaints. Kingdon notes that feedback can reveal a number of problems. First, feedback can show that program implementation does not match legislative intent. Second, it can show a program has not met any of its stated goals. Third, it can show a program has grown too costly. And, lastly, feedback can demonstrate unanticipated and often negative externalities stemming from a program.

Taken together, indicators, focusing events, and feedback describe the various pathways through which problems reveal themselves. However, MSF emphasizes that the objective features of problems matter only insomuch as they are integrated into larger problem narratives. Kingdon (2003) emphasizes that all problems are, for lack of a better term, socially constructed in that indicators, focusing events, and feedback require interpretation and framing vis-à-vis problem definition, a term broadly describing the process through which individuals, organized interests, and policymakers assign meaning to social issues. Kingdon emphasizes that conditions are more or less private troubles whereas problems are conditions that are believed to require government attention. Problem definition is the process through which conditions are translated into problems.

To this end, recent MSF research has underscored the critical importance of problem brokers or individuals that help "frame conditions as public problems and work to make policy makers accept these frames" (Knaggård 2015: 450). Because problems are constantly competing with one another for space on the crowded government agenda, problem brokers help draw attention to issues that, at least in their eyes, were previously ignored and are thus deserving of policymaker attention. The problem stream is said to be ready for coupling when there is a significant deterioration in indicators; a dramatic focusing event or, in some cases, a series of dramatic focusing events (O'Donovan 2017); or feedback that has attracted policymaker attention.

2.2.2 Policy Stream and Policy Entrepreneurship

Kingdon (2003) describes the policy stream as a "primeval soup" where different ideas interact and compete with one another across time. Those ideas deemed worthy of closer consideration float to the top of the soup, while those deemed less worthy drop to the bottom. Ideas are vetted through a process known as "softening up," which describes the assessment and subsequent winnowing down of different policy alternatives within the policy stream.

But who determines an alternative's "worthiness"? That task is delegated to the policy community which is "a loose connection of civil servants, interest groups, academics, researchers and consultants (the so-called hidden participants), who engage in working out alternatives to the policy problems of a specific policy field" (Herweg 2016: 132). The structure and composition of a policy community can have a profound impact on the trajectory of an idea through the policy stream. Research suggests more tightly integrated policy communities, which refers to policy communities that are smaller and more consensual, tend to gradually gestate (or process) new ideas but rapidly gestate old ideas. By contrast, more loosely integrated communities, which tend to be larger and more competitive, tend to rapidly gestate new ideas but gradually gestate old ones (Durant and Diehl 1989; see also Zahariadis 2003).

MSF further argues that certain "criteria for survival" are ever-present during the evaluation of alternatives. For example, all policies are evaluated based on their technical feasibility, which broadly describes the likelihood that an alternative will accomplish whatever it sets out to do. Moreover, policies need to be "compatible with the values" of a given policy community in order to be adopted (Kingdon 2003: 132). Alternatives also need to be financially viable and, to the extent possible, experts within the policy community must believe that the public (and policymakers) will accept the ideas that they're proposing. Lastly, path dependence can influence an idea's survival in that existing policies may constrain the types of ideas entertained by the larger policy community (Spohr 2016; Zohlnhöfer and Huß 2016). The policy stream is ready for coupling (i.e., successful coupling is more likely once a policy window opens) if a viable policy alternative exists, which fulfils most or all of these criteria.

Not all members of the policy community are alike. MSF, which is one of the few policymaking theories to explicitly highlight the role of individuals in promoting agenda-setting and policy change, identifies policy entrepreneurs as important catalysts for change. Policy entrepreneurs are individuals who invest considerable time, energy, and resources (e.g., financial and political capital) to promote policy change. Policy entrepreneurs are important for two reasons. First, they work out policy ideas, present them to other members of the policy community, and seek to get the backing of the policy community by amending their "pet proposals." Second, they help couple the streams. Kingdon emphasizes that savvy entrepreneurs "lie in wait" until the three streams are ready for coupling, at which point they will capitalize on fleeting opportunities to promote agenda change (Kingdon 2003).

Policy entrepreneurs vary in terms of their professional characteristics. They can be government insiders (e.g., high-ranking bureaucrats, elected officials, street-level bureaucrats) (Carter and Scott 2010; Arnold 2021) as well as government outsiders (e.g., issue advocates, industry representatives, academics) (Arieli and Cohen 2013; Bakir 2009). In fact, entrepreneurs need not be individuals at all: studies suggest entire organizations can be characterized as policy entrepreneurs (Dolowitz and Marsh 2000; Schön-Quinlivan and Scipioni 2017).

To be successful, entrepreneurs must be dogged in their pursuit of policy change and skillful in their coupling of the three streams. Most notably, entrepreneurs must be adept at attaching their pet solutions to problems in order to attract elected officials willing to champion their ideas (Kingdon 2003; Zohlnhöfer 2016). To this end, the literature suggests entrepreneurs tend to exhibit certain critical traits, including high social acuity (Balla 2001; Mintrom and Norman 2009; True and Mintrom 2001), strong coalition building skills (Arieli and Cohen 2013; Béland and Cox 2016; Mintrom and Norman 2009), a keen sense of the best way to frame and define issues (Kingdon 2003; Zahariadis 2003), and a knack for gathering and disseminating information (Anderson, DeLeo and Taylor 2020).

Connectedness, broadly understood, is an important predictor of success when it comes to policy entrepreneurship. On the one hand, policy entrepreneurs who wield a prominent position within a particular policy community tend to have greater influence over other members of said community (Novotný, Satoh, and Nagel 2021). On the other hand, policy entrepreneurs with greater access to elected officials and other decision-makers are more likely to be successful in facilitating agenda-setting and policy change (Kingdon 2003).

2.2.3 Political Stream

In contrast to the policy stream, the political stream does not operate at the level of the policy subsystem but at the macro-level of the political system. Hence, the modus of interaction between actors also differs. While the members of the policy community debate the advantages and pitfalls of specific proposals and seek to convince others of their ideas (often through persuasion), Kingdon (2003: 159) characterizes interactions in the political stream as "bargaining." The political stream essentially is about who is willing to politically support a given proposal and who will oppose it – and how strictly. Hence, the main question is whether there is enough political support for a solution from politically relevant actors to make it on the agenda. The relevant political actors (in a wider sense) are the government and parliament and changes in their composition, interest groups, as well as what Kingdon calls the "national mood." Only if policymakers deem the support among these actors sufficient (and opposition as not prohibitively fierce) are they likely to move on with a proposal.

Kingdon (2003: 146) defines the national mood as "the notion that a rather large number of people out in the country are thinking along certain common lines." The national mood essentially reflects a perception of policymakers and their aides. It is these actors who sense the national mood. If they believe the national mood is in favor of a given project, they are much more likely to go with that proposal, while a national mood considered skeptical toward a project makes it substantially more difficult to get that project on the agenda. Importantly, according to Kingdon (2003: 148), the national mood is not necessarily reflected in opinion polls. Rather, he reports policymakers grasp the national mood from different forms of communication with their constituencies or in media editorials. Hence, again and much like in the problem stream, the perceptual element is important in this concept. What counts for a proposal's chances to make it on the agenda is policymakers' perception of the national mood – and not the quasi-objective public opinion from surveys – because this perception is likely to guide them in their decision if they want to move on with a proposal.

Interest groups and their (potential) campaigns are the second element of the political stream. It goes without saying that a proposal is more likely to make it onto the agenda the more interest groups support it and the more powerful these interest groups are. Clearly, if all interest groups back a project, it will be much easier for that idea to make it on the agenda than if all interest groups oppose it. Things are rarely as simple as that, however. Frequently, some interest groups support a proposal while others oppose it. In these cases, policymakers are expected to calculate a "balance of support" (Kingdon 2003: 150). So, again, MSF focuses on the perception of the relevant actors and not any objective facts. Hence, if policymakers or people around them believe that interest group opposition to a project is strong, they may shy away from pursuing it further – even if the perception turns out to be erroneous later. If, however, they think (wrongly or correctly) that interest group support suffices, they are more likely to continue with the project. According to Kingdon (2003), perceptions of interest group strength are not random but are related to resources and intensity. Hence, interest groups that control many resources like financial means, members and the like, are considered more powerful than interest groups with fewer such resources. Intensity, in contrast, has to do with how regularly an interest group deals with the issue at hand. The more regularly an interest group talks about an issue, the more likely it "counts." One could add an element of connectedness. Interest groups that are entitled to be heard (think about some neo-corporatist systems) or enjoy informal access to people in and around government are probably also considered more important by people in and around government than outsider groups.

Finally, the political stream also contains governments and legislatures. For example, some projects might fit the ideology of a particular government or party better than other proposals. Hence, that government is more open toward the proposed idea and the idea stands a better chance to make it on to the agenda than a competing proposal. Similarly, individual ministers can make a difference – even in otherwise identical governments. Hence, if a new minister comes into office, they may be more receptive toward a given proposal than their predecessor. The same is true in principle for members of parliament. Therefore, turnover in the composition of a government and/or parliament is likely to have an important effect on agenda-setting. Similarly, new top bureaucrats can make a difference. Finally, the political stream also deals with turf battles within the administration.

In any discussion about when the political stream is ready for coupling, two issues need to be considered (the following is based on Herweg, Zahariadis, and Zohlnhöfer 2023). On the one hand, the three elements of the political stream – national mood, (campaigns of) interest groups and (turnover of) government and legislatures – may point in opposite directions. The national mood may be enthusiastic about a proposal, but the government may be reluctant to adopt due to ideological concerns and interest group opposition. Is the political stream ready for coupling in this situation? Herweg, Huß, and Zohlnhöfer (2015) have suggested considering government and legislature as the most important element of the political stream because ultimately it is these institutions that have to adopt a policy change (see also Zahariadis 2003). At the same time, according to Herweg, Huß, and Zohlnhöfer (2015), governments or legislatures are, to some extent, influenced by the other two elements of the political stream (depending on the political system under consideration; see Section 4): a national mood considered as enthusiastic toward a project might even induce a skeptical government to become receptive, while a government initially open toward a proposal might have second thoughts when it perceives that most relevant interest groups are hostile. Nonetheless, it is possible that a government will ignore a skeptical national mood or interest group resistance and moves on with the proposal. Hence, it takes center-stage in the political stream.

On the other hand, it is important to keep in mind what readiness for coupling means with regard to the political stream. Importantly, it does *not* mean that the majorities needed for policy adoption are already forthcoming. It is possible – and indeed happens quite regularly – that a proposal makes it on the agenda, but majorities in parliament or the consent of other actors with veto power are not yet certain, but need to be mobilized. The gathering of majorities in many cases only happens during the decision-making phase of the policy process (for details, see Section 3.1). That is not to say, however, that the political stream is irrelevant during agenda-setting. In order for the political stream to become ready for coupling, an actor with some leadership position in government or parliament like a minister or an influential member of parliament – a role Herweg, Huß, and Zohlnhöfer (2015: 446), following Roberts and King (1991: 152), call "political entrepreneur" – needs to actively support the relevant project and demonstrate a willingness to seek agreement for it from all actors with veto power (Zohlnhöfer 2016). Note that political entrepreneurs can also be policy entrepreneurs, but they do not have to come from the policy community. Rather, they may come onboard only when the policy proposal is already considered a viable policy alternative. Instead, their task is to make the project's adoption happen, which they should be able to do given their political leadership position. In conclusion, for the political stream to be ready, it is not necessary that majorities are forthcoming, but that a political entrepreneur is convinced of the proposal and seeks to get it adopted during decision-making.

2.2.4 Policy Windows and Coupling

Having the three streams ready for coupling is a necessary, but not always sufficient, precursor to agenda-setting. Rather, the coupling of the three streams and elevating the proposal onto the agenda becomes more likely only at particular points in time, which John Kingdon has called policy windows. He defines these points in time as a fleeting "opportunity for advocates of proposals to push their pet solutions, or to push attention to their special problems" (Kingdon 2003: 165). While the term "policy window" was introduced by Kingdon in his original formulation of the approach and taken up in much of the literature, we follow recent suggestions (Herweg, Huß, and Zohlnhöfer 2015; Herweg, Zahariadis, and Zohlnhöfer 2023) to add some nuance to the terminology on policy windows. Although we keep the term "policy window" as a generic term, we use the term "agenda window" for opportunities to get proposals on the decision agenda (i.e., for the kind of policy windows Kingdon had in mind). We distinguish agenda windows from opportunities to get policies adopted during decision-making, which we call decision windows (for details, see Section 3.1).

Agenda windows that allow a specific project to move onto the agenda are usually rare and often do not remain open for very long. They can open in the problem and the political streams, but not in the policy stream. In the problem stream, a (series of) focusing events (e.g., natural disasters or terrorist attacks), substantially worsening indicators (e.g., skyrocketing crime rates or dramatically increasing greenhouse gas emissions), or scathing feedback (e.g., a report revealing widespread failures in program administration) can open an agenda window. In the political stream, agenda windows can open if the government changes, a minister is replaced, or the composition of the legislature changes. In these cases, new policymakers may look for new projects, which they can pursue and could therefore be receptive for other proposals than their predecessors. Additionally, a substantial shift in the national mood can also help open an agenda window.

A third and much less prominent way agenda windows can open is through spillover (Kingdon 2003). Spillover describes instances wherein the ascension of one issue onto the agenda substantially increases the likelihood of related issues coming onto the agenda. This can be the case because the first issue helps establish a principle that can be applied to other similar issues. Moreover, there are political reasons for spillovers. Specifically, policymakers may try to reap the political benefits of a successful idea by transferring it to a different issue area. Other times, spillovers occur because a change in one issue area necessitates change in another area. Ackrill and Kay (2011) suggest calling this latter kind of spillover an endogenous spillover, in contrast to the "exogenous" spillovers Kingdon describes.

While some agenda windows are unpredictable (e.g., windows opened in the aftermath of a natural disaster), others are more foreseeable. Elections, the timing of which is usually known some time in advance, bring in new members of parliament who are open to new ideas, for example. Similarly, budget negotiations that occur regularly and usually according to a clear timeframe may open agenda windows for various projects which policy entrepreneurs may seek to use.

The literature has distinguished between different sizes of agenda windows (see Keeler 1993). Landslide election victories or severe crises, particularly those that endanger a government's reelection (see Herweg, Huß, and Zohlnhöfer 2015), are expected to open large policy windows that can be used to promote many and far-reaching agenda changes. By contrast, narrow election victories or less dramatic problems tend to open smaller policy windows that can be used for fewer proposals.

Nonetheless, it is important to emphasize that whether a development turns out to be an agenda window for a specific policy project is not something that can be known or perfectly anticipated in advance. Policy entrepreneurs who advocate for a policy idea may consider a development a window and may seek to use the development to advance their project; however, they still need to convince policymakers that the time for change has come. Sometimes, policy entrepreneurs, thanks in large part to their manipulation skills, are able to take advantage of "unlikely" windows (i.e., developments that are only remotely related to their idea) while in other cases even "obvious" policy windows go unused.

Hence, agenda windows provide opportunities that policy entrepreneurs may or may not fully capitalize on. More specifically, agenda windows provide them with an opportunity to couple the three streams. Hence, coupling is a core aspect of the MSF (for a thorough discussion, see Dolan and Blum 2023). Indeed, once the three streams are ready for coupling and an agenda window opens, policy entrepreneurs should seek to couple the three streams. Partial couplings, that is, couplings of two streams, for example of a policy with a problem, often take place even before a window opens (Blum 2018; Dolan 2021). But the likelihood of getting an issue on the agenda increases tremendously if all three streams can be linked at the same time once an agenda window opens – a phenomena known as "final" or "complete" coupling (cf. Blum 2018; Dolan and Blum 2023).

Agenda coupling essentially means that policy entrepreneurs argue that a given policy proposal promises to solve a pressing problem and that adoption of the policy is at least possible politically (see Blum 2018 and Möck et al. 2023).

Policy entrepreneurs will present their arguments in the most convincing way by emphasizing those elements of the issue at hand that reflect favorably on their project while ignoring other facets that fit less well.

At the same time, policy entrepreneurs must take into account in which stream the agenda window opened to couple the streams successfully. If the window opens in the problem stream, consequential coupling (Zahariadis 2003) takes place. Remember that agenda windows in general and problem windows in particular tend to close very quickly (Keeler 1993). Hence, there is usually no time to work out an entirely new solution and, consequently, existing alternatives will be considered. Under these circumstances, it is particularly important for policy entrepreneurs to explain to policymakers that the policy proposal put forward is particularly well-suited to solve the problem at hand.

Things look slightly differently if the window opens in the political stream. Consider a newly elected government. Presumably, the newly elected government will seek to pass laws fulfilling some of its election promises. Hence, the policy stream will be flush with proposals and the new government will seek out problems to attach their ideas to, a phenomena labeled "doctrinal coupling" by Zahariadis (2003). Finally, spillover windows also operate according to the logic of doctrinal coupling because here, again, the solution that spills over from a different issue area exists and needs to be coupled to some problem. Dolan and Blum (2023) call this phenomenon "opportunistic coupling" (see also Zahariadis 2003).

Two things are noteworthy here. First, in both (or all three if we count "opportunistic coupling") ways of coupling, there is no particularly close correspondence between the problem and the policy proposal that get coupled. Evidently, "everything cannot be connected with everything else" (Kingdon 2003: 222), but there is substantial leeway as to which solution can be considered suitable for a given problem. Second, in both (or all three) coupling strategies, the three streams are not coupled simultaneously. Rather, in the case of consequential coupling, policies and problems are linked first and politics comes in later. In the case of doctrinal coupling, in contrast, the policy and politics streams are coupled first, and the problem stream comes later. This fits nicely with Dolan's (2021) argument about multiple partial couplings. Dolan maintains that sometimes, when a classic final coupling of all three streams for a single issue is impossible, policy entrepreneurs can use multiple partial couplings of different, but related, issues to get their issues on the agenda.

So far, we have argued that policy entrepreneurs seek to sell their pet proposals to policymakers when agenda windows open. Ackrill and Kay (2011) take issue with this conceptualization arguing that policymakers do not necessarily passively wait for policy entrepreneurs to present their proposals.

While not denying that this may happen, they hold that policymakers may also actively look for suitable solutions and select the solution (and policy entrepreneur) themselves.

2.3 Main Hypotheses

Herweg, Zahariadis, and Zohlnhöfer (2023) articulate nine MSF hypotheses on agenda-setting in the *Theories of the Policy Process*. Table 1 lists and defines these hypotheses. It also highlights a number of studies that can be used to help inform the testing of these hypotheses. Note that the list of relevant studies is by no means exhaustive. Nor do all of these studies *explicitly* test MSF hypotheses, although all of them explore topics germane to the various concepts associated with each hypothesis.

3 Extending the MSF's Scope: New Stages of the Policy Process and the Extent of Reforms

The previous section introduced the basic assumptions and core elements of the MSF, particularly as they relate to the framework's explanation of the agenda-setting process. In this section, we discuss a number of suggestions from the literature to expand the MSF's scope. We explore recent attempts to extend MSF to other stages of the policy process including decision-making, implementation, and termination. This section specifically explores the extent to which the MSF is able to shed new light on these processes and how it may need to be adapted for these purposes. It closes by briefly introducing a more recent trend in MSF research which seeks to explain not only agenda-setting and policy changes, but also the scope or extent of these reforms.

3.1 Stages of the Policy Process

It is true that from an MSF perspective there "is no policy cycle in which policymakers identify problems, formulate solutions, and make a choice in that order. Instead, by the time policymakers pay attention to a problem it is too late to develop a technically and politically feasible solution from scratch" (Cairney 2018: 211). Why should scholars seek to extend the MSF to stages of the policy cycle then? There are two reasons for this. First, we follow a terminological trajectory of the literature (also in the MSF tradition, as we will see in this section), which continues to talk about these stages. Second, while problem definition, generation of alternatives and agenda-setting may not necessarily be distinct stages in a linear process (Cairney 2018: 205), proposals usually make it on the agenda before they can be adopted and policies can only be implemented after they are adopted. Hence, the policy cycle heuristic seems to map some

Table 1 MSF hypotheses on agenda-setting.

Hypothesis	Wording in *Theories of the Policy Process*	Relevant Studies
H1: *Entire Framework*	Agenda change becomes more likely if (a) a policy window opens, (b) the streams are ready for coupling, and (c) a policy entrepreneur promotes agenda change	Zahariadis 2003 Zohlnhöfer 2016 Herweg 2017 Koebele 2021 Van den Dool 2023b
H2: *Problem Stream*	A problem broker is likely to be more successful framing a condition as a problem the more an indicator changes to the negative, the more harmful a focusing event is, and the more definitely a government program does not work as expected.	Knaggård 2015 Birkland 1997 O'Donovan 2017 DeLeo 2018
H3: *Political Stream*	Policy proposals that fit the general ideology of a government or the majority in a legislature have a better chance of gaining agenda status.	Travis and Zahariadis 2002 Zohlnhöfer 2016 Herweg 2017
H4: *Selection Criteria* (Policy Stream)	If a policy proposal does not fulfill the selection criteria, the likelihood of gaining agenda status, and thus being coupled, decreases significantly	Spohr 2016 Zohlnhöfer 2016 Van den Dool 2023b
H5: *Policy Communities* (Policy Stream)	As the integration of policy communities decreases, it becomes more likely that entirely new ideas can become viable policy alternatives.	Novotný, Satoh, and Nagel 2021 Zahariadis 2003 Herweg 2016

Table 1 (cont.)

Hypothesis	Wording in *Theories of the Policy Process*	Relevant Studies
H6: *Problem Window* (Windows)	The policy window opens in the problem stream as a result of at least one of the following changes: change of indicators, focusing events, or feedback.	Dolan 2021 Dolan and Blum 2023 Möck et al. 2023 Herweg 2017 Babayan et al. 2021 Van den Dool 2023b Taylor et al. 2023
H7: *Problem Window #2* (Windows)	The more a condition puts a policymaker's reelection at risk, the more likely it is to open a policy window in the problem stream.	DeLeo and Duarte 2022 Ackrill and Kay 2011 Zohlnhöfer 2016 Dolan 2021 Heaphy 2022 Van den Dool 2023b Ceccoli and Chen 2023
H8: *Political Window* (Windows)	The policy window opens in the political stream as a result of at least one of the following changes: changes in the legislature, election of a new government, interest group campaigns, or a change in the national mood.	Herweg et al. 2022 Ackrill and Kay 2011 Herweg 2017 Van den Dool 2023b
H9: *Policy Entrepreneur*	Policy entrepreneurs are more likely to couple the streams successfully during an open policy window if (a) they have more access to core policymakers and (b) they are more persistent.	Anderson et al. 2020 Zohlnhöfer 2016 Mintrom 2019 Herweg 2017

empirical regularities well and recent scholarship has found that while processes at different stages are interdependent, it makes sense to keep them distinct (e.g., Fowler 2022).

3.1.1 Decision-Making

Kingdon's original book only dealt with agenda-setting. Building on seminal work by Zahariadis (1992, 2003), Herweg, Huß, and Zohlnhöfer (2015; see also Herweg 2013) have proposed extensions that make the MSF applicable to the analysis of decision-making. In contrast to other suggestions (see Howlett, McConnell and Perl 2015), Herweg, Huß, and Zohlnhöfer's proposal leaves MSF's operating structure intact and only expands it to a further stage of the policy process. They suggest distinguishing between an agenda window, which is exactly the same as Kingdon's policy window (i.e., an opportunity to get a proposal on the decision agenda), and a decision window. As discussed in the previous section, the agenda window provides policy entrepreneurs with an opportunity to couple their pet proposals to a relevant problem and get the backing of a political entrepreneur. Herweg, Huß, and Zohlnhöfer (2015) call this process "agenda coupling." Once agenda coupling succeeds and the issue is on the decision agenda, the decision window opens and a process called "decision coupling" begins. During decision coupling, the political entrepreneur supplants the policy entrepreneur as the most important actor in the policy process.

What happens during decision coupling? Once an issue is on the decision agenda, the main task is not to couple policy proposals and problems – that already happened during agenda coupling – but rather to find the necessary majorities to get the proposal adopted. Hence, the political stream takes center stage during decision coupling, although, as we will see, the other two streams remain relevant. Stitching together majorities may not always be a particularly difficult task. If the proposal is backed by the leader of a majority party in a Westminster system or the dictator in an autocracy, this support might be enough to secure policy adoption. In systems with various veto actors (e.g., presidents, second chambers, governing coalitions or referenda), the path from the institutional agenda (agenda-setting) to the statute book (policy change) is wrought with pitfalls. Moreover, interest groups may launch campaigns against the proposal, further complicating the policy adoption process.

Under these circumstances, political entrepreneurs often need to win the consent of these veto actors. The literature highlights a number of strategies political entrepreneurs have at their disposal when building consensus among veto actors (see Herweg, Huß, and Zohlnhöfer 2015; Zohlnhöfer, Herweg, and, Huß 2016). First, they can offer concessions by supporting the adoption of a diluted version of their preferred policy. In many cases it may be easier to get small-scale changes, rather than large-scale changes, adopted (Zohlnhöfer 2009). Indeed, political entrepreneurs may believe enacting small-scale changes will open the door for additional changes in the future, a strategy that Zahariadis (2003) has called "salami tactics." What is more, Kingdon (2003: 191) explains that small changes may establish a principle by setting a precedent that alters the way policies are discussed in a particular policy area. Hence, political entrepreneurs may be more than willing to accept concessions if they can get the principle of their policy established.

Package deals are yet another strategy for securing the passage of a proposal during decision coupling. Recall that the MSF argues that there are almost always several solutions that can be coupled with one problem. Political entrepreneurs can take advantage of this fact. If they cannot find the necessary majority for a specific proposal (say a tax cut to mitigate a recession), they can add other proposals from the policy stream (e.g., a spending increase) to their bill to widen legislative support. Moreover, political entrepreneurs by definition occupy political leadership positions and therefore are usually well connected to other issue areas. Hence, they can strike package deals across issue areas by, for example, supporting somebody else's health-care reform in exchange for the backing of their own tax proposal.

Third, political entrepreneurs can try to manipulate policymakers. On the one hand, a political entrepreneur can go back to the problem stream and look for indicators, focusing events, or feedback that make the problem to which their favorite policy proposal has been coupled look particularly grave.[6] On the other hand, institutional manipulation may be used, which refers to situations wherein political entrepreneurs work to centralize decision-making by circumventing relevant actors. Examples include political entrepreneurs threatening to resign should their parties not follow their preferred course of action, the European Commission putting legal pressure on individual member states to broaden its support coalition, and a top bureaucrat sidestepping the opposition of interest groups via international negotiations (Herweg 2017; Turaga and Mittal 2023; Zohlnhöfer 2016).

Modifying the framework in this way also allows to take into account the effect of political institutions (Zohlnhöfer, Herweg, and Huß 2016), thereby addressing the long-standing criticism that the MSF fails to consider institutional constraints (Mucciaroni 2013; Rüb 2014; see also Bolukbasi and Yıldırım 2022). While political institutions seem less relevant during agenda-setting,

---

[6] This manipulation strategy is not only available for political entrepreneurs seeking to find majorities for their proposals, however. It may also be possible that decision coupling is stalled because the problem fades away or competing policy entrepreneurs are able to de-couple policy and problem.

their importance substantially increases when we analyze decision-making (see Baumgartner et al. 2009), a testament to the fact that institutions define whose agreement is required for the adoption of a law. Put in MSF parlance, institutions define whose agreement a political entrepreneur must obtain during decision coupling. In this regard, there is a huge difference between places like the United Kingdom, where one party holds a majority in a quasi-unicameral system without any further veto actors, and the United States or Switzerland with their intricate systems of checks and balances. In the former systems (and many autocracies), decision coupling is often a smooth process. Once a political entrepreneur from the governing party (or, in case of an autocracy, the ruling elite) supports a proposal it typically becomes law, unless, of course, an interest group campaign or lack of party/elite cohesion manages to derail passage. The strategies of political entrepreneurs will be much more relevant in systems with many veto actors since majorities often need to be put together by manipulation, package deals, and concessions. Moreover, the adopted policy often looks remarkably different from the original proposal.

These arguments about decision-making from an MSF perspective also allow us to deduce a number of hypotheses (see Herweg, Zahariadis, and Zohlnhöfer 2023 for details), some of which predict the likelihood of policy adoption. For example, adoption becomes more likely if the political entrepreneur holds a formal government position, if there are no other actors who could veto the proposal, if package deals are feasible, if policymakers can be manipulated by pointing to a highly salient problem, or if the decision-making process is highly centralized. Other hypotheses deal with the degree to which veto actors and interest groups are likely to alter an original proposal during the decision-making stage: The more actors have veto power, the more likely a proposal will be altered. Similarly, the more powerful interest groups are that oppose a proposal, the more likely that concessions will have to be made.

3.1.2 Policy Implementation

Scholars have also used the MSF to investigate policy implementation, although there is a lack of consensus regarding what, exactly, the term "implementation" means in the context of these studies (Herweg and Zohlnhöfer 2023). Some researchers use the MSF to investigate how lower-level actors in multilevel settings respond to higher-level decisions, which they have to transpose ("implement") into the lower level's law (the transposition of EU directives by member states, the regional adoption of federal laws, etc.) (for Switzerland, see Sager and Thomann 2017; Sager, Rüefli, and Thomann 2019).

These instances of "implementation" can be regarded as cases of policymaking in multilevel settings; however, and, as we will show in Section 4, no huge conceptual adaptations are necessary in these cases.

Other scholars have instead focused on executive policymaking, most notably the carrying out of policies by administrative agencies (see for example Boswell and Rodrigues 2016; Exworthy and Powell 2004; Goyal, Howlett, and Chindarkar 2020; Howlett 2019; Ridde 2009; Taylor, Zarb, and Jeschke 2021; Zahariadis and Exadaktylos 2016; Zahariadis and Petridou 2023; see Herweg and Zohlnhöfer 2023 as an overview that summarizes many of these studies). Many of these authors substantially amend the original MSF, adding, dropping or replacing streams. While the various scholars who study policy implementation from an MSF perspective take note of each other and cite each other, their approaches are very different and do not seem to lead to a common MSF perspective for explaining policy implementation.

Luke Fowler (2019, 2022, 2023) offers the most promising approach to explaining policy implementation from an MSF perspective. Fowler leaves the framework's operating structure untouched, explicitly engages MSF's assumptions, and provides a convincing explanation of how ambiguity shapes policy implementation. Fowler's starting point is that adopted policies are often ambiguous, in part because package deals and compromises are needed to build majorities, in part because controversial issues may be covered by formulaic compromises that can be interpreted differently by different actors, and in part because many policies are purposefully left incomplete to mitigate conflict during the adoption stage. Despite the seemingly inherent murkiness of the content of policies, implementers have to make sense of these compromises to make implementation work.

According to Fowler (for the following see Fowler 2023: chapter 1, in particular) all three streams remain relevant during implementation, but some amendments are necessary. The policy stream, for example, is no longer the province of competing ideas and proposals. Rather, it consists of the various possible interpretations of adopted – but still ambiguous or incomplete – policies. These interpretations are worked out in interactions of implementers (not dissimilar to interactions in policy communities). Policy interpretation must fulfill certain criteria of "technical, financial, and political viability" (Fowler 2023: 43), which is, again, reminiscent of the criteria for survival in the policy stream for agenda-setting. This means that not all interpretations of the law are possible, and policymakers can shape these criteria by stipulating certain administrative procedures. Similarly, these criteria are also shaped by organizational culture and incentives.

In principle, the problem stream consists of the same conditions policy-makers use to identify problems in need of change. The problem stream is important during implementation because the success of a policy can be assessed based on the extent to which it mitigates the problem it was originally created to solve. Implementers are most likely to focus on problems that are clearly defined and have unambiguous indicators. If, however, more than one problem is addressed by the policy or there are no clear and uncontroversial indicators of the problem, then implementers have much more room for interpretation, meaning they can strategically focus on some problems (or elements of a problem) while ignoring others.

Regarding the political stream, it is unlikely that policymakers, given their time constraints and problematic preferences, will pay attention to implementation unless the policy returns to the public eye, either because it does not work or because the national mood or changes in government have altered policymaker expectations. Should any of these things happen, implementers are likely to change the way they implement the policy in accordance with these expectations.

Implementation windows typically open as a policy is being adopted. Only rarely do changes in the problem stream – for example, a focusing event suggesting that implementation must be amended – or the political stream – for example, a new government requests a different administrative process – open an implementation window. If all three streams are ready for coupling, because there is an interpretation of the policy that requires change in implementation behavior, because there is a problem indicator that demands action, or because the national mood or the government support implementation, then a change in implementation behavior will occur. Otherwise, implementers are unlikely to change their implementation behavior on their own accord.

If adopted policies are open to (re-)interpretation during implementation, then those entrepreneurs who were successful during the agenda-setting and decision-making stages will want to make sure their interpretation of the policy continues to prevail. In contrast, policy entrepreneurs who were unsuccessful during the earlier stages may try to use the ambiguity of policies to de- or re-couple the streams during implementation by coupling their interpretation of what the problems is and how it should be handled to the policy that was adopted (see also Zahariadis and Exadaktylos 2016).

Hence, the MSF can be a highly enlightening lens when investigating policy implementation. Moreover, as Fowler (2022, 2023) points out, connecting agenda-setting, policy adoption, and implementation in an MSF perspective promises highly fruitful insights. Empirical research should take up this perspective in the future.

3.1.3 Policy Termination

Policy termination is a rare event (Geva-May 2004; Wenzelburger and Thurm 2023). Many programs are continued despite the fact that they are not needed anymore or fail to attain their goals. Therefore, policy (non)termination does not fit the view that policymaking is an exercise in orderly problem-solving – just as policy formulation does not often follow that logic. MSF is thus an excellent candidate for analyzing policy termination (as already argued by Geva-May 2004), although only few scholars so far have applied it to questions of policy termination save Wenzelburger and Hartmann (2022).

Conceptually, the abolition of policies should not pose an overly vexing problem for MSF. Indeed, policy termination is similar to policy adoption: both need to make it on the decision agenda and both require approval by veto actors (Wenzelburger and Thurm 2023). Evidently, policies that are to be terminated are viewed as problematic. Indicators, feedback or focusing events likely pointed at problematic consequences or a lack of efficiency or effectiveness of a policy before termination ensued. Likewise, changes in government or the national mood (core elements of the MSF's political stream) are also important factors that are regularly alluded to in the literature on policy termination. In short, neither the problem nor political streams require major adaptions to explain termination.

Things are slightly different for the policy stream. Prima facie one could think that if a policy is to be abolished, then the policy stream could be irrelevant because there is no new policy that needs to be softened up. Upon closer inspection, however, it becomes clear that some of the criteria for survival are highly relevant when it comes to policy termination. Terminating a policy has just as many consequences for the real world as policy adoption and policymakers need to conjecture what those consequences will be. In the case of policy termination these consequences have to do with the fallback position or the legal status of an issue once a policy is terminated. Consider the termination of a tax law. Since the abolition of a tax law may result in lack of revenue, policymakers have to consider whether termination is financially feasible. Hence, the fallback position is of prime importance in the policy stream and MSF analyses of policy termination need to investigate thoroughly if the fallback position satisfies the criteria for survival. Similarly, Wenzelburger and Thurm (2023) also note that the procedural aspects of dismantling a policy may become important in the policy stream, namely, questions of timing and compensation for beneficiaries of the policy to be terminated.

"Termination windows" do not differ significantly from agenda windows. Similar to agenda-setting, policy termination is more likely to make it on the agenda if a window in the political or problem stream opens. Moreover, many policy terminators are similar to policy entrepreneurs in that they frame issues and seek to convince policymakers and the public that terminating a policy will be beneficial (Wenzelburger and Thurm 2023). Nonetheless, in some cases, "outside terminators" (Geva-May 2004: 329) are identified in termination studies. Outside terminators are persons from outside the policy community who are in charge of implementing the policy. To the extent that these actors can hope to be particularly successful because they have some experience with the policy to be terminated, they may be particularly trustworthy – but still remain policy entrepreneurs. If, however, these actors are in charge of getting the termination decision implemented (Wenzelburger and Thurm 2023), they only become relevant after abolition of the policy and they resemble policy implementers (see previous section). In sum, it seems that the MSF can also be applied fruitfully to policy termination and hence can cover most stages of the policy cycle.

3.2 Scope and Scale of Reform

Most MSF research discusses if and when an agenda change occurs or when policy changes. Moreover, sometimes scholars also investigate in which direction the respective change might go (Herweg 2013). MSF research has largely overlooked questions regarding the scope and scale of policy reforms, however, a curious omission given that this topic has been investigated in various competing theories. For example, the Advocacy Coalition Framework (Nohrstedt et al. 2023) distinguishes between minor and major policy change and seeks to explain which causal paths lead to one versus the other. The Punctuated Equilibrium Theory's (PET) core idea is to differentiate between the determinants of large-scale policy change ("punctuations") versus smaller scale or incremental changes (Baumgartner, Jones, and Mortensen 2023). Finally, the Veto Player Theory (Tsebelis 2002) is interested in the potential for the size of policy change (i.e., the size of the "winset") as well. The MSF, by contrast, mostly remains quiet about the size of change apart from a few scattered arguments about the effects of the size of policy windows and the structure of policy communities on the extent of reforms (see Keeler 1993; Zahariadis and Allen 1995).

This is not to say, however, that MSF has *nothing* to say about this topic. Rather, Zohlnhöfer (2023) has argued the MSF indeed lends itself to explaining when large-scale reforms are likely to make it on the agenda and when we will only observe incremental agenda and policy change. Various factors induce incremental change. One, of course, is that no policy entrepreneur advocates far-reaching change. That could be the case for many routine decisions like the adjustment of tax codes or welfare state replacement rates to inflation (in cases where such an adjustment does not take place automatically). Apart from these uncontroversial routine decisions, every element of the MSF can potentially explain why only minor changes (or no changes at all) breach the agenda or get adopted. For example, if a focusing event opens a policy window and policymakers feel they have to respond but there is no acceptable alternative in the policy stream, then they may content themselves with a very moderate change. Put differently, they have responded to the focusing event but did not risk adopting a policy that was not softened up in the policy stream. Similarly, if opposition to a proposal in the political stream is substantial, policymakers may prefer a watered-down version of their policy in order to limit potential electoral risk. Moreover, some problems (e.g., climate or demographic change) are "big, slow-moving and invisible" (Pierson 2003). These problems may be very important in the future, but they rarely produce dramatic focusing events that would trigger a response. While these issues are discussed politically and hence policymakers might want to respond, they are unlikely to invest a lot of political capital into these issues unless the national mood demands action. Finally, veto actors can demand concessions during decision coupling which could also lead to less far-reaching reforms.

In contrast, to observe major agenda and policy change, all three streams must be ready for coupling, a policy window must be available for the issue at hand, and veto actors who wish to block the proposal must be absent. Nonetheless, even under these conditions major change is not necessarily forthcoming. Rather, it is essentially the policy window that makes far-reaching change happen (see also Keeler 1993). Take problem windows as an example. If problems are skyrocketing and acute, doing nothing is unlikely to be an option, so policymakers may prefer to do more rather than less and hence adopt large-scale policy change. Similarly, in acute crisis situations that are difficult to make sense of (think of the initial stages of the COVID-19 crisis), credible problem brokers or policy entrepreneurs may have an easier time convincing policymakers that major changes are needed. Similarly, when a new government forms after a landslide election victory or the national mood is considered to overwhelmingly support a proposal, major changes are also more likely. Finally, following PET logic, if an issue has been neglected for a long time, the changes necessary to fix the problem might be particularly large – and hence large-scale change becomes more likely.

Given the recency of these arguments, it is not surprising that they have yet to be tested empirically. It is possible, however, to deduce a number of MSF hypotheses on the scale of change that lend themselves to systematic testing in the future (see Zohlnhöfer 2023). While these hypotheses may not hold all of the time, they demonstrate that the MSF, in principle, is capable of explaining the extent of agenda and policy change.

3.3 Conclusions

This section explored recent attempts to move MSF beyond the agenda-setting stage of the policy process. While we could not present every proposed MSF modification, the ones we discussed suggest the MSF holds up fairly well across the various stages of the policymaking process. Indeed, we have discussed all stages of the policy cycle (recall that feedback is part of the problem stream during agenda-setting) and found that, at least conceptually, the MSF promises to shed new light on decision-making, policy implementation and policy termination. Similarly, the MSF also seems able to go beyond the questions of if, when, and how agenda or policy change occurs and to inform about why, in some instances, large-scale reforms are adopted while, at other times, only incremental change is possible. In many cases, authors have also deduced hypotheses from the MSF (in its respective modified versions) that can be tested empirically. Given that many of these extensions have been published only recently, many have not been tested empirically – at least not sufficiently to assess their empirical validity. Nonetheless, even if individual hypotheses may eventually be falsified, that will also advance the framework as it will likely lead to more nuanced reformulations of hypotheses or the discovery of factors that have not received sufficient attention hitherto. What, however, will be necessary, is a reliable empirical approach to test the MSF and its hypotheses which uses valid operationalizations of the framework's key concepts, a topic we return to later in the Element. The next section will examine the extent to which MSF can be extended not to new stages of the policy process, but to new policymaking contexts, countries, and levels of government.

4 MSF in International Contexts

In addition to extending MSF into new stages of the policy process, researchers have also sought to apply the framework to political systems outside of the United States. Scholars have successfully used the MSF to explain policymaking in various political contexts, including other presidential systems (e.g., Latin America), parliamentary systems, and authoritarian systems. Moreover, MSF has also been applied to international or supranational organizations like the European Union, which are somewhat detached from domestic politics and where policymaking plays out very differently than in nation states. Similarly, the MSF has been applied to multilevel political systems where domestic and international policy processes interact. The MSF is able to provide interesting perspectives on all of these levels; however, modifications are needed in order to make the framework applicable. The following section reviews some of this research.

4.1 Latin America

As we have seen in Section 1, the MSF has not been widely applied to Latin American countries. *Prima facie*, Latin American governments should not pose significant problems for an MSF application because these systems mostly resemble the United States in that they are presidential. However, closer analysis reveals a number of notable differences that necessitate modifications to the framework.

Three particularities of Latin American systems are relevant when applying the MSF to the region (Sanjurjo 2020b, 2023). First, in most Latin American systems, the executive dominates policymaking while the legislative and judicial branches play a more subordinate role. Second, because Latin American parties tend to be weak, Latin American party systems often fall short of delivering adequate representation. Complicating matters further, the bureaucracy is often unable to design and implement suitable policies. In turn, interest groups play a more significant role in policy development. Finally, given the extreme levels of inequality in many Latin American countries, the national mood is polarized and exerts comparatively little effect on policy-making as it is considered "indifferent" (Sanjurjo 2023: 162). The weak institutionalization of political parties and the importance of clientelism also help explain why the national mood only plays a minor role in these political contexts.

With these distinctions in mind, Sanjurjo (2020b, 2023) argues that, although the problem and policy streams can essentially remain unchanged, the political stream requires modification when applied to Latin American states. Rather than focus on all three elements of the political stream (national mood, organized political forces, and government), Sanjurjo specifically advises focusing on what he calls the "presidential coalition" or the group of political allies that help the president to get policies adopted. Furthermore, interest groups have heightened influence given the weakness of political parties. Although the national mood should not be dismissed entirely, according to Sanjurjo, it is only of secondary relevance. Thus, MSF travels well to Latin America, although some amendments, particularly to the political stream, seem appropriate – an observation we will make in other contexts again.

4.2 Parliamentary Systems

Policy processes in parliamentary systems may seem more "orderly" at first glance (Zahariadis 2003: 1) than the presidential system of the United States. Policy processes are often more centralized in these settings due to the strong position of the government that commands a parliamentary majority. Moreover, parliamentary systems used to be populated by cohesive parties with somewhat coherent policy profiles, which should make MSF's assumption of problematic policy preferences less plausible.

Nonetheless, many empirical studies have successfully applied the MSF to policymaking in these systems, in part because problems are just as complex and ambiguous in parliamentary systems as they are in presidential systems. Nor is there anything in the functioning of parliamentary systems that makes the emergence of policy communities any less likely than in presidential systems. Policies need to be developed in both systems. And, with respect to the political stream, party ideology may suggest the broad direction of policymakers' preferences but still leaves ample room for policy entrepreneurs to manipulate elected officials and other actors. Moreover, since voters have become more volatile and catch-all or cartel parties have proliferated, parliamentary systems have evolved in ways that make them even more amenable to MSF (see Herweg, Huß, and Zohlnhöfer 2015).

A number of modifications have been suggested to improve the MSF's explanatory power in parliamentary contexts. Starting with Zahariadis (1995), many scholars have underscored the importance of comparatively cohesive political parties in parliamentary systems and proposed to amend the makeup of the political stream accordingly (for the following see Herweg, Huß, and Zohlnhöfer 2015). Accordingly, parties are mostly interested in putting policies on the agenda that reflect their programmatic preferences and help them get elected. Thus, policy entrepreneurs will have an easier time getting issues on the agenda when they demonstrate that these policies belong to issue areas where voters consider the governing parties to be competent, namely, issue areas these parties are assumed to "own." Governing parties will not be able to restrict the agenda to these issue areas, however (Green-Pedersen and Mortensen 2010).

On the one hand, the national mood may favor projects in issue areas the governing parties cannot claim ownership over. While they might try to keep these issues from the agenda, this will not always work, and, consequently, the government will be forced to deal with these issues as well. Hence, those policies that policymakers believe are backed by the national mood are more likely to make it on the agenda – even if the governing parties do not "own" these issues. On the other hand, the prospect of interest group mobilization in opposition to a proposal can keep governing parties from pursuing a policy, especially if they fear the counter-mobilization will put their reelection at risk. Hence, even if parties are the most relevant actors in the political stream, the stream's other elements still remain relevant (Herweg, Huß, and Zohlnhöfer 2015).

What happens if the elements of the political stream point in opposing directions? Herweg, Huß, and Zohlnhöfer (2015) argue that governing parties – and their evaluation of how given problems and policies are likely to impact their (re)election chances – ultimately determine the trajectory of an issue in these cases. For example, if the national mood is assessed as supporting a project, then a project may crack the agenda even in the face of interest group opposition. Other times, projects may make it on the agenda despite a lack of public or interest group support. This can happen if the governing parties believe that the policy – unpopular as it may be among many interest groups and the majority of the voters – is the best way to deal with the problem and that the persistence of the problem will jeopardize their reelection in the future. In turn, governing parties may calculate that it is better to move ahead with their pet proposals even in the face of public and interest group opposition in the immediate term.

Note that this argument does not rely on clear policy preferences on the part of policymakers. It is not necessary to assume the project they pursue is going to solve the problem: policymakers only need to *believe* that it will. Nor do we have to assume that policymakers are capable of accurately assessing their reelection prospects. Rather, they may judge their reelection chances on the basis of intuition, their reading of the national mood, or opinion polls. It is entirely possible that their assessment is inaccurate. All that matters is that they *believe* their reelection is in jeopardy.

While the political stream needs to be adjusted for parliamentary systems, the problem stream does not typically need to be amended. Herweg, Huß, and Zohlnhöfer (2015) do suggest, however, a slight modification of the policy stream. Once again, the different roles of political parties in parliamentary versus presidential systems lie at the heart of this suggestion. Political parties in parliamentary democracies used to be fairly policy-oriented, meaning they used to adopt different programmatic stances into public policies (see, for example, Budge and Keman 1990). Although these patterns may have become substantially weaker in the twenty-first century (Potrafke 2017), parliamentary parties are still fairly "hands on" with respect to the development of policy alternatives. They are far less likely to delegate the development of policy alternatives to experts compared to parties operating in presidential systems. In fact, parties' policy experts will be active members of the policy community.

In some cases, these party experts act as policy entrepreneurs themselves, developing policies and seeing them through the softening-up process. In other cases, party experts are the target of entrepreneurial activity and policy entrepreneurs will work to convince the party policy experts of the soundness of a particular proposal. This fairly nuanced distinction suggests a need to modify our conceptualization of the softening-up process so that it now takes place *within* parties. In both cases, however, proposals that can be linked to a long-standing programmatic position of a party are more likely to be taken up than policies that deviate from the core positions of that party.

We can thus conclude that the MSF seems to travel well to parliamentary systems. The political stream may need some amending, but, similar to the case of Latin America, the relevant categories are already there. And, while some modifications of the policy stream have been suggested, they leave the operating structure of the MSF completely unaltered.

4.3 Autocracies

While different types of nondemocratic systems can be distinguished (Cheibub, Gandhi, and Vreeland 2010; Geddes, Wright, and Frantz 2014; Wahman, Teorell, and Hadenius 2013), most tend to share a number of common features: (1) a lack of contested elections; (2) considerable restrictions on media freedom and societal pluralism; and (3) a high degree of centralization of political authority (Alvarez et al. 1996; Jones, Epp, and Baumgartner 2019). The MSF's main assumptions have shown to hold up in autocratic regimes; however, all three streams need to be amended to apply the framework to non-democracies (for the following see Herweg, Zahariadis, and Zohlnhöfer 2022).

Starting with the problem stream, a higher number of problems are likely to be ignored in autocratic versus democratic states. Moreover, autocratic states likely harbor certain biases with respect to the types of problems that government should attend to. This is because autocratic regimes are often highly centralized and media freedom is limited or even absent, making it difficult for problem brokers to generate attention for a specific condition. The media are unlikely to take up an issue unless the ruling elite allow them to[7], and it usually takes time for the autocratic center to be informed about a problem on the ground. Furthermore, even if the autocratic center learns about a condition that could be made a problem, agenda change is not necessarily forthcoming. Rather, autocratic governments will find it easier than democratic

---

[7] There is some evidence that social media can be used to flag problematic conditions in autocracies (e.g., Wu 2020). These possibilities are limited, however, because autocracies also impose restrictions on social media.

governments to ignore issues given the enormous restrictions on media free-dom. Autocratic leaders may be less fearful of critical questioning about their (lack of) response to a problem. Moreover, absent free elections, policy nonresponse does not have (immediate) political consequences even if the public is dissatisfied.

Hence, autocratic governments are likely to selectively respond to problems. While they could be highly attentive to issues related to their ideological core, they tend to ignore conditions that could be interpreted as signs of the system's failure. Of course, not dissimilar to democratic leaders, autocratic regimes will almost always deal with those problems that put regime stability or the political survival of the dictator at risk.

The policy stream requires surprisingly few modifications when applied to autocracies. Policy communities in autocracies share similarities to the highly integrated communities found in some policy domains in Western democracies (Zahariadis and Allen 1995): they are small, rather consensual, and conflict is muted due to restricted access as members are picked by the autocratic elite. The main difference between autocracies and democracies regarding the policy stream is that in nondemocracies the "anticipated approval of the current leader" (Herweg, Zahariadis, and Zohlnhöfer 2022: 213) is by far the most important criterion for survival. Because changes in government can be extremely rare in autocracies, waiting for the next election to find a more receptive government is rarely an option for policy entrepreneurs operating in autocratic contexts. The overriding importance of this criterion is likely to lead to the exclusion of many otherwise suitable policy alternatives (Liu and Jayakar 2012). In contrast, other criteria for survival, like financial viability and technical feasibility, take a back seat in nondemocracies.

The political stream likely requires substantial modifications in autocracies, a testament to the fact that the establishment of interest groups is often substan-tially restricted, there are no contested elections (which implies that policy-makers do not need to take the national mood into account), and changes in government are rare. In short, the autocratic elite dominates policymaking. Once the dictator supports a proposal, the proposal has a high likelihood of adoption. But the dictator cannot take care of every issue, and, in many cases, political entrepreneurs (e.g., individuals from ministries or the ruling party) will be responsible for policy development. Hence, policy entrepreneurs, in most cases, will need the backing of a political entrepreneur who will then seek support among the ruling elite. Moreover, while changes in government are much rarer in autocracies (e.g., when a new leader comes in), when they do happen, they likely have far-reaching consequences. At the same time, turnover is much more frequent at lower levels (higher ranks of the ruling party or the ministry), which might also lead to receptivity to new ideas (e.g., Sieleunou et al. 2017).

While it is true that the autocratic leadership dominates the political stream, and interest groups and the national mood only play minor roles in shaping agenda-setting processes, we should not completely exclude these factors from consideration. To the extent that interest groups exist, their position may be taken into account by the autocratic leader. Moreover, even in highly unfree societies, like current China or Nazi-Germany, there is/was evidence that some form of a national mood was taken into account (Herweg, Zahariadis, and Zohlnhöfer 2022). More important than the national mood, however, is what has been termed the "selectorate's mood" (Herweg, Zahariadis, and Zohlnhöfer 2022: 216). Following Bueno de Mesquita et al. (2003), one could argue that a dictator's survival hinges less on their support among the general public but rather on the support of the selectorate, namely, the group of people who have the right to choose the leader, or the winning coalition. Hence, a project may be more likely to get on the agenda if the mood of the selectorate supports it.

Just like elsewhere, policy windows in autocracies can open either in the problem stream – particularly if a condition jeopardizes regime stability or the dictator's political survival – or in the political stream – for example, if a new autocrat comes in, new ministers and top bureaucrats take office, leading positions in the party are filled with new people or the selectorate's mood changes. Accordingly, while some modifications seem in order to make the MSF applicable to the analysis of autocratic regimes, the framework seems surprisingly well suited to explain policy processes in these settings. Herweg, Zahariadis, and Zohlnhöfer (2022) have deduced a number of MSF hypotheses specifically for autocracies. It is noteworthy that these hypotheses correspond quite closely to those that scholars have come up with in analyses of individual autocratic cases (in particular van den Dool 2023a, 2023b and Babayan, Schlaufer, and Uldanov 2021).

4.4 European Union

The MSF has been widely applied to EU policymaking (Herweg and Zahariadis 2018; Herweg and Zohlnhöfer 2022; see also Richardson 1996; Zahariadis 2008). The assumptions on which the MSF is built seem to fit the political system of the EU quite well. Take the EU's committee system as an example, which seems to approximate the assumption of unclear technology. The members of any one committee know quite well what they are doing, but they usually do not fully comprehend their committee's role in the overall decision-making process (Herweg and Zahariadis 2018). Participation is fluid at the EU level as the Council of Ministers meets in different formations depending on the issue area under consideration. Thus, there is considerable variability in terms of the membership of relevant decision-making bodies at any given moment. Moreover, any change in government or of a minister in any of the twenty-seven member states changes the composition of the respective Council (Herweg and Zahariadis 2018). Finally, Ackrill and Kay (2011) argue that the MSF's core concept of ambiguity applies to the EU's institutional arrangement because, while each Directorate-General has a specific thematic focus, issue areas overlap while "lacking a clear hierarchy" (Ackrill and Kay 2011: 75). This somewhat paradoxical arrangement amounts to what the authors call "institutional ambiguity."

This said, because the European Commission is active in the policy, political, *and* problem streams, the EU, in some respects, may contradict the assumption of stream independence (Herweg and Zahariadis 2018). Nonetheless, the fact that an actor is present in more than one stream does not per se mean that stream independence is violated. Rather, the relevant question is whether stream dynamics differ, i.e. if, for example, negotiations continue to prevail in the political stream while argument remains the dominant mode of discussions in the policy stream. If that is the case, stream independence is not violated despite the important role of the European Commission in all three streams.

Scholars have offered a number of adaptations to apply the framework to the EU (Ackrill and Kay 2011; Bache 2013; Copeland and James 2014; Herweg 2017; Saurugger and Terpan 2016; Zahariadis 2008). Like in the previous cases, the political stream has received most of the scholarly attention. Nonetheless, and quite unfortunately, there is little agreement between scholars as to which elements of that stream should be amended – and how (see Herweg and Zahariadis 2018; Herweg and Zohlnhöfer 2022). Herweg's (2017) modifications are perhaps the most encompassing since they amend all three streams while retaining most of the key components of MSF's original structure (see also Herweg and Zohlnhöfer 2022).

The national mood is translated to encompass the European mood, a term broadly describing how EU-level policymakers perceive the European publics' preferences on different issues. Whether such a European mood exists or not is an empirical question, however. The variety of languages in the EU together with the fact that the attention of voters, parties, and media is focused on the domestic level despite the enormous importance of the EU should caution researchers to assume a European mood without giving reasons to believe it exists in their respective field of study. In contrast, there can hardly be any doubt that interest groups matter a great deal at the EU level. Rather, it is important to keep in mind that European interest groups coexist with purely domestic ones, creating a multilayered system of advocacy.

The role of government and parliament is more intricate. Naming the functional equivalents on the European level is not particularly difficult (European parliament as parliament and European Commission, Council of Ministers, and European Council as government), but how can we assess these institutions and their actors' receptivity to different proposals? Whereas partisan affiliation is used as a proxy for policymaker preferences at the domestic level, ideological cohesion of parties at the EU level is low. Zahariadis (2008: 518) observes that a policymaker's national affiliation likely matters. For example, some countries are more "pro-European" than others, which makes them more sympathetic to European proposals. Moreover, the costs of transposition for any given proposal will differ across countries, thereby creating another potential predictor of preferences that looks quite different from partisan affiliation.

With respect to the problem stream, minor modifications are necessary. First, feedback is likely to be more frequent in the EU since many EU legal acts contain review clauses mandating routine monitoring (Hahnkamper-Vandenbulcke 2022). Second, problem brokers operating at the EU level must first ensure the EU retains legal jurisdiction over the items that they seek to draw attention to. The EU is constrained in terms of its authority and may only pass legislation in the areas specified in the EU Treaty (principle of conferral).

Nor does the policy stream require significant adjustments. Policy communities comprise actors operating at both the EU and national levels of government. Moreover, the European Commission often plays an outsized role in the policy stream at least in comparison to domestic legislative institutions (Zahariadis 2008). In fact, the Commission can, in some instances, initiate the creation of policy communities at the European level, a notable departure from domestic policymaking (Herweg 2016). Furthermore, while the criteria for survival are, in principle, applicable at the EU level, they are weighted differently than in domestic contexts. One notable example is the criterion of tolerable costs, which will differ considerably by country. As such, some authors have suggested this criterion be omitted (e.g., Zahariadis 2008).

Scholars have yet to observe any substantive differences with respect to when the problem and policy streams are ready for coupling at the EU level. However, Herweg (2017) convincingly argues the political stream is ready for coupling if the European Commission supports a proposal. Nor does the framework need to be modified to explain windows opening in the problem stream. Windows in the political stream open with elections to the European Parliament, when a new Commission takes office, or with a swing in the European mood (if it matters for the respective project) – hence, these mechanisms are similar to the original

MSF as well. Moreover, the regular summits of the European Council may also open political windows. The same applies when the Commission or a new Council presidency release their specific work programs. The preparation of these documents may also provide an opportunity to get an issue on the agenda.

In sum, while some modifications are evidently necessary to apply the MSF to the EU, these amendments are relatively moderate and the operating structure of the framework clearly remains untouched. At the same time, once the MSF is adequately adapted, it is a particularly promising lens for the analysis of policymaking processes at the EU level, as can be read off many successful extant empirical applications.

4.5 Multilevel Systems

The EU is a good example of multilevel policymaking, as the governments of member states are involved in supranational policy formulation while at the same time they must respond to EU legislation domestically. Federal states are also multilevel systems, although the need for interaction between the federal and the state levels varies considerably by country. Moreover, multilevel policymaking takes place when countries interact in international negotiations or international organizations where they seek to shape common policies by disseminating their ideas, but also (have to) adopt policies domestically that they have agreed upon at the international level (see Rietig 2021, 2023).

Extant literature suggests MSF requires a number of modifications before being applicable to multilevel contexts (Bache 2013: 34; for the following, see Knaggård and Hildingsson 2023). When analyzing the problem stream, it is evident that some problems are not confined to a single country or jurisdiction but rather are transnational. Examples include climate change, migration, and emerging disease policy (Rietig 2021). These problems affect various levels, and hence, problem brokers can seek to bring these problems to policymakers' attention at various levels – either at the same time or by targeting those levels most receptive to their problem definition.

But even if problems can, in principle, be dealt with at the national level, multilevel dynamics can play a role. For example, comparative indicators collected at the higher level by organizations like the World Health Organization, the Organization for Economic Co-operation and Development, and the EU can flag domestic problems. Indeed, Kingdon (2003: 111) observed that when one country's performance is believed to be "falling behind" other countries, there may be domestic calls to close the gap. The more systematically higher levels produce these kinds of league tables, the more likely it becomes that a country will discover that others are doing better in a particular issue area and that something needs to be done. Similarly, since many policies in federal states are implemented at lower levels, it is likely that feedback from these lower-level units can help spotlight a problem. Finally, it is plausible that focusing events at one level of government can elevate a problem onto the agenda of a different level. Additionally, problem brokers may experiment with or learn new framing tactics at a lower level that they can then apply to their advocacy efforts at a higher level (see Knaggård and Hildingsson 2023).

For the policy stream, it is important to take into account the fact that policy communities are increasingly becoming transnational, meaning they comprise experts from various levels of government (see Bache 2013; Rietig 2023). Alternatively, members of the policy community on one level look for ideas at other levels (Goyal 2022; Lovell 2016). One important aspect of looking for "'tried and tested' policy solutions" (Lovell 2016: 766) from other levels (or other jurisdictions) is their effect on the criteria for survival. If a proposal has been implemented successfully elsewhere, the criteria of technical feasibility and financial viability should be much less controversial (Goyal 2022).

There are some peculiarities regarding the political stream under conditions of multilevel policymaking. Lower-level policymakers can be members of higher-level decision-making bodies, like in the EU Council of Ministers. Multilevel systems may also allow for venue shopping by policy entrepreneurs, assuming more than one level has jurisdiction (Knaggård and Hildingsson 2023; Rietig 2021). Furthermore, a discussion of an issue at one level can increase the salience of an issue at another level (Goyal 2022), hence increasing the likelihood that the political stream at the other level becomes ready for coupling. Finally, if a higher level adopts a policy that the lower level has to respond to, doing nothing is no longer a possibility at the lower level, in turn changing the power distribution in the political stream in ways that favor change (Goyal 2022).

Finally, multilevel dynamics can also have implications for the opening of policy windows (see Knaggård and Hildingsson 2023). For example, focusing events elsewhere may open problem windows. While this mechanism is not necessarily confined to multilevel systems, the mechanism is more likely to operate in these settings. Similarly, political windows can also open at multiple levels. Think of the results of regional or European elections that sometimes open policy windows at the national level. Potentially, policy decisions at a higher level may also open policy windows at lower levels, such as in the case of European directives that have to be transposed into national law by the member states. As noted earlier, some scholars consider this an example of policy implementation. However, given that the lower-level decisions are very similar to regular policymaking processes and are very different from processes of bureaucratic implementation, we think they should be considered as examples of multilevel policymaking.

In sum, the MSF is able to shed light on policymaking in multilevel settings. While some amendments seem in order to explain these processes, the basic structure of the MSF can, again, remain unchanged. Moreover, Rietig (2021) shows how international and domestic dynamics co-evolve and interact. Hence, she expects that agenda-setting at a higher level, for example the conclusion of an international agreement, will make decision coupling more likely at a lower level, like legislation transposing the agreement into national law, which in turn can induce further agenda change at the higher level.

4.6 Conclusions

This section provided an overview of the attempts to apply the MSF to political systems outside of the United States. With some slight modifications, most of which do not touch on the operating structure of the framework, it is possible to adapt the MSF to different kinds of polities, from the presidentialism of Latin America to the parliamentary systems of Western Europe (and elsewhere), from autocracies to intricate multilevel policymaking and complex supranational organizations like the EU. By all accounts, MSF travels extremely well, although the degree of adaptation needed to successfully apply the framework obviously varies depending of the policymaking context. Not surprisingly, the political stream often requires the most significant adjustments – a testament to the enormous social, cultural, and institutional differences shaping political behavior in each state and within each system. With these extensions in mind, the following section takes a closer look at the various strategies scholars can use to systematically apply the framework and rigorously test core hypotheses.

5 Methods and Analysis

While the MSF has been widely applied and found to be useful, empirical studies have not all followed rigorous designs and analytical methods (see, for example, Cairney and Jones 2016). We use the term "rigor" as a general call to apply methods well as part of the broader need for policy scholars to be more systematic, transparent, and explicit in how they collect and analyze the information used to produce the findings being reported. We explicitly do not advocate for the use of any one analytical method. Our rationale is inspired by Weible and Workman (2022: 1) who note that a focus on methods is "notably absent in policy research," resulting in limited theoretical growth in the study of the policy process. We convey this message by alerting MSF scholars to the need to employ methods that are explicit, systematic, and transparent.

That's what we mean by "apply methods well." Thus, we propose strategies for systematically conducting an MSF study: operationalize the MSF elements and employ rigorous analytical techniques to exploit the MSF's potential to its fullest (the following builds on Zohlnhöfer, Herweg, and Zahariadis 2022).

Of course, it all starts with a good research question. While the original book by Kingdon (2003) asked why some ideas become prominent on the policy agenda while others do not, subsequent research has extended the scope of the MSF to the entire policy process (see section 3). Consequently, the MSF can also be applied to answer questions of policy change, such as, why does a policy get adopted or what factors make its successful implementation more likely and why? Similarly, the MSF can be used to explain the extent of a reform (Section 3).

Next, the author must specify time and space. Are they conducting a comparative study? If so, what design should be used? If a single case study, how well are alternative explanations discounted? One of the better expositions of the methods that could be employed with the MSF is still Kingdon's (2003) original study. Although it employs a time frame that will not suit most analysts (four years of data collection), Kingdon goes through methodological problems and solutions very carefully and articulates interesting ways to capture the essence of many MSF concepts.

Following these steps comes the development of hypotheses. Specific MSF hypotheses were spelled out in previous sections, so we will not repeat that discussion. Suffice it to say, we aim to show in this section how to measure the MSF elements and not whether they are linked to outcomes in some way.

5.1 Operationalization of MSF Elements

As noted in previous sections, the MSF conceptualizes policymaking as the result of interacting five elements: the three streams (problems, policies, and politics), policy windows, and policy entrepreneurs. Each stream flows relatively independently of the others and obeys its own dynamics. Therefore, the logic of analysis needs to operationalize the elements/items of each stream and then measure if each stream is ready for coupling before the important phase of coupling can be investigated.

5.1.1 The Problem Stream

The problem stream consists of public problems that preoccupy the attention of social groups or policymakers. Public problems contain a perceptual element (Kingdon 2003) in that they need to be perceived as problems by a large portion of the public or policymakers. Depending on the research question, *indicators* are one way to operationalize problems. For example, if labor or social policy is of interest, unemployment figures in percentages are important measures of problems. If economic growth is of analytical interest, percentage change in gross domestic product is a useful indicator. Of course, simply reporting the current level of unemployment is of little analytical interest. The key is to compare changes over time or, if germane to the research question, across countries and to show that significant changes are causing difficulties. In addition, it is important to show the contours of the problem frame. For example, whether social unrest is framed as an unemployment or economic growth problem makes a difference. It is incumbent on the analyst to show evidence that specific (not general) problem frames are capturing attention mainly through interviews, public testimony, or media articles. The analysist must demonstrate the observed indicator changes are being debated, investigated, and so on.

Focusing events are another way of identifying problems. For example, natural or man-made disasters, such as earthquakes or terrorist attacks, may, in some instances, point to inadequacies of policy resilience that should be addressed. Pointing to gaps between needs and capabilities does not mean there is one way of framing these problems or even that there is wide agreement on what the problem is. For example, Birkland (2004) notes that the aftermath of the September 11, 2001, terrorist attack brought about significant changes in multiple sectors partly because different groups framed their "problem" in ways that dovetailed the event and captured policymaker attention. There were economic problems, like company survival among airlines; airport security problems; and, of course, broader intelligence failures and domestic surveillance problems. Analysts must not only specify numerically or qualitatively through interviews or other qualitative sources the focusing events but also draw clear lines to the way they affected and limited problem frames. It is not enough to say 9/11 happened and therefore airline survival problems ensued. One must also specify the emergence of airline performance frames via interviews with officials, testimonies before Congress, company documents, and other sources of qualitative material.

Feedback is yet another problem arousal mechanism. Feedback from assessment tools provides clues as to successes and failures of programs. For example, a mid-term assessment report of the first Greek bailout program identified recalcitrance to implementing the austerity because of the huge political cost associated with them. It became apparent that the Greek political elite was part of the (but not the only) reason why the program did not yield the expected benefits (Zahariadis 2013). Feedback may be captured by reports and interviews and measured in terms of deviations from stated goals. Here again it is imperative that the research not only demonstrate the existence of a particular source of feedback (e.g., a report) but that the report somehow permeated policymaker – and perhaps even public – consciousness to shape awareness and framing of a particular problem.

5.1.2 The Policy Stream

Items in the policy stream are ideas or solutions floating in what Kingdon called the "primeval soup." They are essentially solutions that are being worked out in policy communities. Depending on the research question, scholars need to identify what these communities are, their membership, and the dynamics that facilitate the emergence of some solutions but not others. The choice of the dependent variable determines which part of the policy stream receives attention and which part can be neglected. For example, studies of agenda-setting may not need to capture the dynamics and structure of the entire policy stream including the long softening-up trajectory of all alternatives. Rather, it may suffice to specify the short list of ideas, which survived the softening-up process.

As stated in Section 2, policy communities are groupings of participants and interested experts in each policy sector. They go beyond epistemic communities and include what, in the United States, are called "iron triangles" of policy-makers, the bureaucracy, and interest groups. Members can be identified through surveys, media coverage, or interviews. Especially helpful is the "snowballing" technique whereby researchers ask interviewees to identify important actors in the community. When no new names come up, the researcher can be reasonably certain that all members are accounted for. Moreover, scholars can use these data to investigate the structure of the policy community with the help of network analysis (Novotný, Satoh, and Nagel 2021).

Three factors (or criteria for survival) make it more likely that ideas will become serious contenders for policy consideration when the time comes: technical feasibility, value acceptability, and budgetary implications. Technical feasibility refers to whether proponents have worked out the details of how the new program – if one is involved – will be implemented. For example, is there administrative capacity (agencies, human capital, etc.)? Expert discourse or parliamentary hearings are ways to air out these issues and for analysts to assess this criterion. Value acceptability refers to an option's receptivity among policy community members. Do they speak in favor of it? Does it speak to their sense of efficiency, effectiveness, or equity? Media coverage and interviews, think tank reports, academic discourse, and survey research provide a fine-grained glimpse of such debates within the community. Budgetary cost is a special consideration. Does the proposed number of resources needed for successful implementation exist? Is it appropriate relative to the budget climate? For example, a proposal to create a new agency in times of high budget deficits is less likely to survive this process.

A proposal does not need unanimous (or even majority) backing in the policy community to be considered a viable policy alternative (see Zohlnhöfer, Herweg, and Zahariadis 2022 for details). So how do we know there is support? If many members come out in favor of it, then a researcher can safely infer there is adequate support. If many policy experts are undecided and do not explicitly support one policy proposal, acceptability is low and no viable policy alternative likely exists. In this instance, coupling should be difficult.

5.1.3 The Politics Stream

The politics stream consists of three elements: the ideology of government and parliament, the balance among interest groups, and alignment with the national mood. Do these elements support the rise of an issue on the governmental agenda or favor the idea's adoption?

Because policymakers are assumed to have unclear preferences, ideology is often used as a rough criterion to gauge policymaker receptiveness at the macro level. Party platforms or political media proclamations are good indicators for measuring the distance between policymaker predilections and the policy's "spirit." For example, policies that include generous income support for marginalized communities are less likely to find a receptive audience among Republican lawmakers in the United States. Conversely, a pro-business proposal, such as company tax breaks and other fiscal incentives, will likely have more traction in the same Republican circles.

The balance of interest groups reflects organized social pressures for or against certain policies. Press releases, parliamentary hearings, or public action demonstrate this balance in reasonably clear ways. Policymakers gauge such sentiment and formulate positions that often take into account interest group preferences. Of course, just as there are some policy ideas that more closely dovetail a party's platform than others, so too are there some groups that are able to exert more influence over one party versus the other. For example, the National Rifle Association (NRA) is wildly influential in Republican circles, but less so in Democratic circles. It is thus imperative that researchers account for these nuances when assessing the overall effect of interest groups on the politics stream (for details see Zohlnhöfer, Herweg, and Zahariadis 2022).

The *national mood*, defined as "a rather large number of people out in the country (...) thinking along certain common lines" (Kingdon 2003: 146), is another important element of the political stream. As already emphasized in Section 2, the core idea of the national mood concerns policymakers' *perceptions* about what people think. Therefore, Kingdon (2003) explicitly warns against confounding the national mood with the results of opinion polls. Given that policymakers tend to follow representative opinion surveys closely and often even commission them (Herweg, Huß, and Zohlnhöfer 2015), it has been suggested to look at such surveys as one way to measure the national mood (Zohlnhöfer, Herweg, and Zahariadis 2022; see Bundgaard and Vrangbæk 2007; Zahariadis 2015; Sanjurjo 2020a as examples). While this advice remains valid, it should be complemented by as much information on policymakers' actual perception of the national mood as possible because research has shown that policymakers are often far off when judging public opinion (Walgrave et al. 2023).

At the same time, it is unclear if survey respondents always hold preferences that are stable over time and independent of the specific context. Fastenrath and Marx (2023) show that opinions on taxing the rich in Germany are quite malleable in the context of focus group discussions and that the preferences expressed in these interactions in many cases differ widely from the same respondents' answers on related survey questions. Hence, it is at best unclear how robust survey results are when push comes to shove in the political debate. Interestingly, in expert interviews, these authors also find that policymakers are aware of this fact and "discount" the results of opinion polls accordingly. In the actual example, this led left-leaning politicians to refrain from pursuing the agenda of tax-increases despite a prima facie supportive public (according to opinion polls) because policymakers feared that support would crumble substantially once opponents of the proposals would enter the arena – an intuition that was supported in the focus group discussions.

Therefore, scholars should look for as much evidence as possible to determine how policymakers perceive the national mood. There are multiple ways to do so. In a study of renewable energy policy in Hawaii, Kagan (2019) conducted twenty-five interviews with key actors, which allowed her to reconstruct policymakers' perception of the national or, in her case, state mood. Zohlnhöfer (2016) mostly uses written sources, particularly memoirs, to assess how policymakers perceived the national mood regarding German labor market reforms. Dolan (2021) looks at media reporting to analyze the national mood regarding Australian climate change adaptation policy. The systematic analysis of social media or internet search data may be another way to operationalize the national mood, potentially even in autocracies (cf. Schuler 2020).

5.1.4 Policy Windows

Policy windows are opportunities that occur because of sharp changes in either the problem or the politics stream. They constitute the context within which policymaking takes place. Of course, not all windows are created equal. Some are really big windows (Keeler 1993), such as those triggered by focusing events like 9/11, that command attention and color policy for years (Birkland 2004). In general, Herweg, Huß, and Zohlnhöfer (2015) argue that conditions that put a policymaker's reelection at risk are more likely to gain attention. To capture this condition empirically, researchers must make a plausible argument that policymakers believed their reelection chances were threatened by nonaction. For example, Zohlnhöfer (2016) collected evidence to show that the German government under Gerhard Schröder believed that the stubbornly high level of unemployment would endanger its reelection chances. Similarly, Dolan (2021: 177) demonstrates that the serious threat of being ousted triggered Prime Minister Howard's belief that lack of response to the Australian Millennium Draught would endanger his reelection.

5.1.5 Policy Entrepreneurs and Coupling

One of the most innovative aspects of the MSF, as presented by Kingdon (2003), was the incorporation of policy entrepreneurs as agents of change (or the status quo). The idea is to add the element of agency in policymaking to highlight the fluidity and unpredictability of the process. Institutions make things possible, but people make things happen. Policy entrepreneurs are individuals or corporate actors who devote time, resources, and skills to advocate, persuade, manipulate, mobilize, broker, or stymie support for or against policy options.

The first step is to identify who the policy entrepreneurs are. This may be distilled by memoirs, interviews, parliamentary hearings, speeches, social media announcements, and other such sources. For example, Cook and Rinfret (2013) identify Lisa Jackson, the U.S. Environmental Protection Agency administrator, as a policy entrepreneur when analyzing greenhouse gas emission regulation in the United States. They do this by comparing the higher number of her public speeches and addresses on climate change relative to her predecessors. Similarly, in his UK case study on security privatization, Staff (2020) identifies the Labour MP Bruce George as the policy entrepreneur thanks to evidence from expert interviews and the MP's high profile and long engagement in this issue area.

Identifying policy entrepreneurs is important, but operationalizing their resources and negotiating skills is essential to capturing the likelihood of success in policymaking. Resources/characteristics include persistence and access to policymakers. While an exhaustive inventory of negotiating skills – measured indirectly as strategies (Zohlnhöfer, Zahariadis, and Herweg 2022) – has not yet been attempted, some successful strategies include brokering (Knaggård 2015), coalition-building (Zahariadis and Exadaktylos 2016), affect priming (Zahariadis 2015), and framing and the use of symbols (Zahariadis 2003: 14). Strategies may be discerned by observing the actions or rhetoric of entrepreneurs. For example, framing strategies in terms of losses, instead of the government's frame of gains, provided strong clues to Zahariadis (2003) in how the opposition was able to derail the Greek Prime Minister's plans for compromise in Yugoslavia in 1992.

Persistent policy entrepreneurs "spend a great deal of time giving talks, writing position papers, sending letters to important people, drafting bills, testifying before congressional committees and executive branch commissions, and having lunch, all with the aim of pushing their ideas in whatever way and forum might further the cause" (Kingdon 2003: 181). While persistence is relatively easy to discern from interviews and hearings, how does one assess entrepreneurs with access? One way to do this is through social network analysis to identify nodes and intensity of interactions (e.g., Novotný, Satoh, and Nagel 2021; Petridou et al. 2023). In general, access refers to having a claim to a hearing with important politicians or influential people or groups. This claim results from several sources: "expertise; an ability to speak for others, as in the case of the leader of a powerful interest group; or an authoritative decision-making position, such as the presidency or a congressional committee chairmanship" (Kingdon 2003: 180). Hearings, articles, interview sources, or formal position are good ways to discern access. Entrepreneurs who have better access have higher chances of succeeding in coupling.

How do we know when coupling occurs? Although most MSF studies deal with coupling from a systems perspective (the streams are ready, a window opens, and change occurs in the output end; cf. Dolan 2021), others use process tracing (Collier 2011) to address this issue. Sanjurjo's (2020a) case study on gun control policy in Brazil, for instance, traces the actions of policy entrepreneurs. The author shows that once the streams were ready for coupling, entrepreneurs started arguing that their pet project – strict gun controls (policy stream) – would be a good solution for the country's serious problems of violence and homicides (problem stream). Following political support, which they skillfully cultivated through media campaigns, they accessed key policymakers at the state and federal levels (political stream) to forcefully put the item on the agenda. Möck et al. (2023) provide a novel approach for investigating coupling. They code media reports and apply discourse network analysis to analyze the interactions between problems, solutions, and politics.

5.2 Choosing an Appropriate Analytical Technique

There are two ways to collect and analyze data: qualitatively and quantitatively. Both have benefits and drawbacks, and no one is better than the other. It all depends on the nature of the research question. Some scholars advocate the use of multi-methods as a remedy to different drawbacks in qualitative and quantitative research (e.g., Brady and Collier 2010). We maintain an agnostic stance on this issue, preferring a more traditional presentation of each technique separately and urging scholars to consider the technique or combination of techniques that best suits their project. Although most MSF studies tend to be qualitative case studies, there are also some promising statistical (or large-N) analyses.

5.2.1 Qualitative Techniques

Having addressed issues of research design (Gerring 2017; Seawright and Gerring 2008), the next main task is to develop a case study protocol that contains explicit references to variables and ways to collect, analyze, and overcome analytical issues with those variables.

MSF designs must incorporate variance in the dependent variable. The implication is that research must investigate successful and unsuccessful couplings (for a detailed discussion, see Töller 2023). This problem is particularly acute with single cases. But there are ways to address this issue. For example, Venters, Hauptli, and Cohen-Vogel (2012) analyze how the political stream prevented agenda change introducing the U.S. national sales tax for education during the Nixon administration. Similarly, Zahariadis (1996) investigates the attempts at privatization of British Rail by focusing on four political windows and two problem windows between 1974 and 1992. Other studies that look at failed couplings include Münter (2005) and Sanjurjo (2020a). Because of the "too many variables, too few observations" problem, single cases may increase observations by lengthening the time component (e.g., Zahariadis 2005) or compare cases across units and over time within and across cases (e.g., Zahariadis 1995). Rigorous hypothesis testing may also be performed via process tracing (Collier 2011), whereby analysts evaluate and/or eliminate alternative hypotheses using methodologically established standards (see Staff 2020).

A major concern is reliability, that is, ensuring replicability of results. Two strategies for improving reliability include creation of the case study protocol and development of a database (Yin 2018). Relevant documents to be included in a protocol are an overview of the project, field procedures, sources and their appropriateness, guiding questions, and a report outline (see Zohlnhöfer,

Herweg, and Zahariadis 2022 for a template). MSF researchers also need to specify a timeline of events, perhaps by consulting media sources to keep track of what happened and when. The protocol and database help guide data collection, especially interview questions directed at specific interviewees.

When using interviews as the main source of data, care must be exercised to decide who to interview and to ask the "right" questions (Tracy 2019). The sample of interviewees and questions should contain a mixture of relevant public and private actors depending on the research question. For example, interviewees should be members of parliament, agency heads and other civil servants, social actors from relevant interest groups, academics, journalists, and others depending on the issue at hand. The idea is to get relevant information, which then needs to be triangulated with other sources of evidence. Triangulation is important not only because it cuts down on the cost of interviews but also because it provides an important check on the veracity of evidence. People may lie to increase their sense of importance. For example, Zahariadis (2015) notes that in all his interviews Greek policymakers complained of the constraining effects of the national mood (as measured by public opinion). Had some policymakers or other sources in the media reported that public opinion did not matter, that would be cause for more data collection. Triangulation helps identify such discrepancies and increases data reliability.

5.2.2 Quantitative Techniques

Because only two quantitative (or large-N) techniques have been applied so far to MSF studies, regression analysis (DeLeo and Duarte 2022; Goyal 2022; Travis and Zahariadis 2002) and qualitative comparative analysis (QCA) (Sager and Thomann 2017; Shephard et al. 2021), we concentrate on these two here (see Engler and Herweg 2019).

Regression analysis fits well the MSF's probabilistic logic. Three types are appropriate. The first is logistic regression, which calculates the odds ratio of the size of an independent variable's effect (e.g., policy stream) on the dependent binary variable (agenda status: change or stability). However, when change over time is sought, logistic regression analysis does not work well. To model the time dimension more precisely, scholars may opt for event history analysis (Box-Steffensmeier and Jones 1997). This type of regression investigates the effect of the independent variables of interest over time until an event occurs (see Goyal 2022 for an application). Finally, if the dependent variable is continuous, multiple linear regression or pooled time series will work. Using pooled time series and a series of interaction terms to model couplings, Travis and Zahariadis (2002) apply the MSF to explain levels of US foreign aid in the 1980s and 1990s.

However, regression analysis comes with challenges. Notwithstanding the usual concerns of assigning numerical values to, say, agenda items, scholars must be careful with two main problems. First, variance in the dependent variable is imperative. Just like in qualitative research, scholars must account for both agenda or policy change *and* stability. Second, the notion of coupling is modeled mathematically through a multiplicative (interaction) term. Because the MSF contains five core elements, a complete test should assess interactions among all of them plus their independent effects. This results in a high number of variables and interactive terms, which are very difficult to interpret. Engler and Herweg (2019) suggest overcoming this drawback either by condensing the streams' readiness for coupling into one variable or by testing partial couplings only. For example, DeLeo and Duarte (2022) use regression analysis to explore the dynamics of the problem stream and conduct a qualitative case study of the other streams and coupling activities. Dolan (2021) shows the usefulness of partial couplings, which effectively means that, theoretically, one may test manageable two-way interactions.

In contrast to regression analysis, QCA is more limited because it is not a linear model but a set theory based on deterministic logic (Engler and Herweg 2019). QCA analyses can answer which (combination of) factors are necessary/ sufficient for agenda change, for example, but they cannot test for which factor makes change more likely. Resulting from different assumptions about how the dependent and independent variable(s) are causally connected, it is quite evident that QCA does not directly test MSF hypotheses. For this reason, attention should be paid to QCA's consistency value. Consistency informs how many of the cases that exhibit a causal condition are also members of the set of cases that exhibit the outcome. Low levels indicate many such cases (cf. Schneider and Wagemann 2012).

Despite challenges, quantitative techniques provide a good way to test MSF hypotheses. They allow for more precise measurement of impact and help disentangle combined and individual factor effects with greater accuracy over time and across cases. This feature is a vital asset of scholarly research that aims to produce reliable and accurate findings.

5.3 Conclusions

In this section, we have shown how potential MSF studies may be conducted. Starting with a good empirical question and after considering issues of research design, we have argued that it is important to think of ways to measure the different MSF concepts. Our suggestions are merely that, suggestions. There are multiple ways to operationalize concepts, and we referred to several promising ones.

Despite advocating analytical rigor and technique appropriateness, we stress three words of caution with comparative applications. First, greater scope for empirical applications raises the specter of conceptual stretching (Sartori 1970). Applications in many different national environments naturally create problems of conceptual appropriateness. Although there are ways to deal with this issue (Collier and Mahon 1993), the temptation is to adapt the MSF to make it fit the specific circumstances under investigation. This is particularly true in single case studies, which constitute the bulk of MSF applications. We encourage scholars to be mindful of the need for generalizability and conversation beyond their case study. The MSF does not explain every policy decision in every situation. We understand that our argument implies a certain balance between conceptual stretching and outcome explaining, but we contend that this is an empirical question that cannot be settled theoretically. Rigorous testing will show how far the MSF should travel.

Second, we have not touched on operationalization in nondemocracies. The balance of interests, for example, may make a big difference in democratic systems as evidence of social pressures, but does it really affect nondemocracies unless these groups are linked to the ruling elite? In this case, what does operationalization of the concept mean even if one were to argue it has an impact? We could be talking about two different things while using the same terminology. It is essential that scholars define their terms, specify their adaptations (if any), and be explicit about their operationalization.

Finally, while most MSF studies are qualitative methodologically, we believe more quantitative studies are warranted, but with a caveat. Numerical measurement comes at the cost of nuance. For example, the balance of interest groups may be gleaned qualitatively through interviews and other sources of data collection. What does a value of 2 mean in that case? Care should be exercised to ensure that methodological rigor also pays tribute to theory. This point is particularly relevant for the MSF where actors' perceptions of problems, the national mood, the balance of interest, or the fulfillment of the criteria for survival are central for the explanation of agenda-setting and policymaking.

6 Advancing the MSF Research Agenda

This Element provides evidence of the remarkable theoretical and conceptual advancement and innovations in MSF scholarship in recent years. Key concepts have been clarified and better operationalizations suggested, extensions to other stages of the policy process like decision-making and policy implementation have been proposed as have adaptations to other political systems, from parliamentary democracies to autocracies, from supranational organizations to multi-level policymaking. Moreover, we have discussed how to improve MSF case studies and how to test the framework quantitatively. However, despite these important advancements, more work remains. The concluding section seeks to spotlight a number of gaps in MSF research. Our review is by no means exhaustive. We are confident there are other research topics not listed here. Instead, our intent is to spotlight a number of obvious omissions in order to stimulate potentially fruitful research projects. Our discussion of existing gaps and recommendations revolves around axes that account for theoretical and methodological concerns.

6.1 Theoretical Implications

6.1.1 Investigate More Closely the Role of the Media in Agenda-Setting

One of the (potentially) most relevant factors that have not been taken up by MSF scholarship so far is the influence of media (as already observed by Rüb 2014). While Kingdon (2003: 59; italics in original) argued that "[t]he media report what is going on in government, by and large, rather than having an independent effect *on* governmental agendas," many other scholars argue that the media are indeed likely to have an impact on agenda-setting (e.g., Wolfe, Jones and Baumgartner 2013; Sevenans 2018). Indeed, the media are not necessarily neutral transmitters of information but instead select which information is considered interesting to their audience and which is not. Hence, some information has a higher likelihood of being taken up by the media than others; that is, their news value differs. For example, items that contain less complex and more easily communicable information, negative information, and information that is directly relevant to media consumers are expected to be placed higher on the agenda (e.g., Jensen and Lee 2019). Hence, when looking at the problem stream, the chances of turning a condition into a problem can differ depending on the news value of different items.

Similarly, the media can shape policymaker perceptions of the national mood. So, again, given that the media have to select which information they want to circulate, their role can become highly significant in the political stream. Moreover, one further relevant qualification of policy entrepreneurs (in addition to the ones discussed so far in this Element) could be their skills in "playing the media game" or the extent to which they are adept at communicating their message through the media.

Hence, future MSF research should discuss how the mainstream, alternative, and social media can influence agenda-setting and policymaking more generally. It seems plausible that the media play a role in all three streams, but it remains to be uncovered how exactly they can influence the policy process from an MSF perspective. Moreover, it is likely that the way the media system is organized – think of the differences between the polarized U.S. system and the British system with the enormously important publicly funded but independent BBC – may have an impact on how the media affect policy processes. Finally, the ever-increasing relevance of social media also needs to be considered. At the same time, these arguments have to be assessed empirically both qualitatively and quantitatively (for the latter, see Soroka and Wlezien 2019).

6.1.2 Revisit Core Aspects of the Problem Stream

Few aspects of the MSF have received more attention than the problem stream, a testament to the fairly robust sub-streams of research on focusing events and problem indicators. While this work has provided critical insights into the exogenous factors influencing issue attention and agenda-setting, one could argue that it has, as alluded to in Section 2, strayed a bit from Kingdon's original conceptualization of the problem stream in that each of these items is typically examined discretely as opposed to in conjunction with one another.

To be clear, Kingdon does not preclude the possibility that certain domains may be more sensitive to focusing events or indicators than other domains. In fact, there is now a voluminous body of literature suggesting that issue attention in certain domains is either more event-driven (e.g., natural disasters) or indicator-driven (e.g., public health, environmental) than in other domains (DeLeo et al. 2022). However, Kingdon's depiction of the problem stream also implies that this need not always be the case. Indeed, he explicitly notes that sometimes indicators need a nudge from focusing events suggesting both factors may work together to drive issue attention and change. But it is not clear when. This is also consistent with Hypothesis 2 in Section 2, which suggests problem brokers can draw on all three items when rallying attention toward a particular issue. Given these important distinctions, future research is behooved to adopt a slightly more dynamic conceptualization of the problem stream that explores the interplay between all three elements as opposed to the piecemeal approach that tends to dominate extant MSF research.

What is more, even in those domains that have, historically, been assumed to be more indicator- or focusing event–driven, there may be exceptions to the rule. Recent work suggests the temporal dimensions of problems (e.g., their onset, duration, or timing) can blur the conceptual boundaries between focusing event, indicators, and other aspects of the problem stream (e.g., DeLeo et al. 2022; Dolan 2021). The literature demands a more nuanced understanding of some of these concepts. For example, DeLeo et al. (2022) maintain that the pattern of agenda-setting evidenced during the COVID-19 pandemic suggested the crisis was focusing event–driven despite the fact that the problem itself was largely revealed through accumulating public health indicators, namely, cases and deaths.

Lastly, one element of the problem stream that is curiously overlooked is policy feedback. Our analysis revealed few studies explicitly examining the role of feedback in generating issue attention and change. This omission is problematic given the obvious importance of executive agencies in drawing policymaker and public attention to different issues. One potentially fruitful area of research would explore whether different sources (e.g., government versus nongovernment) and types of feedback are more or less likely to help facilitate successful coupling as well as the potential strategies used by problem brokers to convince policymakers of the importance of a particular report's findings.

6.1.3 Carefully Analyze the Selection Criteria in the Policy Stream

A bevy of studies have helped clarify and define the conceptual boundaries of policy communities, which are arguably the single most important element of MSF's policy stream (Herweg 2016). This work has proven instrumental in communicating best practices for identifying the actors comprising policy communities as well as their relative influence in shaping the adoption of different ideas and policies. In turn, it has provided a useful springboard for future studies to further investigate the role of policy communities in accepting/ rejecting different ideas.

But whereas research on policy communities has flourished in recent years, less is known about the ways in which various criteria for survival listed in Section 2 (technical feasibility, value compatibility, financial viability, public acceptance, and path dependence) effect policy acceptance. Zohlnhöfer, Herweg, and Zahariadis (2022) point to the need for researchers to empirically assess whether a particular proposal meets all or at least some of the criteria for survival from the perspective of a policy community. We echo this suggestion but add that it may also be helpful to assess whether certain criteria are weighed more heavily at certain times, in certain contexts, or even in certain domains. For example, it is plausible that disparities in financial resources may make certain policy domains more or less sensitive to financial constraints than others. Moreover, certain policy domains (e.g., economic policy, social welfare policy) tend to engender a more attentive public than others, suggesting potential variability in the extent to which the community closely attends to public acceptance as a criterion for survival. Similarly, we have argued in Section 4 that in autocracies the "anticipated approval of the current leader" is of overriding importance while other criteria have to take a backseat. Alas, these are merely a sample of the various ways in which future research can begin to unpack the way in which criteria are vetted during the policy process.

6.1.4 Carefully Tease Out Implications for Policy Entrepreneurship

One of the more innovative aspects of the original MSF formulation was the concept of policy entrepreneurs. Scholarly interest in policy entrepreneurship has since flourished in its own right as research has explored the role of entrepreneurs as key policy actors (e.g., Mintrom 2019; Petridou and Mintrom 2021), their strategies and action (e.g., Capano and Galanti 2021), and has embedded the concept in other theoretical policymaking frameworks. The MSF has not kept up with these advances. There are at least two possible scholarly directions that research may take. The first concerns the inventory of successful (or not) coupling strategies. While the issue will be settled empirically, theoretical work is needed to ensure that the list of strategies is as exhaustive as possible and that it is not merely a laundry list of strategic behavior but a bounded and theoretically nuanced model of policy action. Do these strategies work in all environments, and, if not, what are the implications for MSF coupling processes?

The second area focuses on identifying different types of entrepreneurs and their aims. A number of research studies have identified new "types" of policy entrepreneurship. For example, recent MSF research has differentiated policy entrepreneurs from so-called political entrepreneurs, noting that political entrepreneurs are typically individuals who hold a position within government and whose support for a policy proves instrumental in facilitating its adoption (Herweg, Huß, and Zohlnhöfer 2015; Asante 2023). Moreover, Petridou et al. (2023) conceive of the existence of reactive versus proactive entrepreneurs and maintain that there is a theoretical implication for the MSF. Proactive entrepreneurs seek out opportunities to couple the streams in the classic MSF conceptualization. Reactive entrepreneurs react to opportunities without preconceived notions. They do not have specific solutions in mind, and their coupling strategies are fundamentally different. Still others have suggested "street-level entrepreneurs," or front-line bureaucrats whose proximity to clients allows them to shape policy outcomes, play a critical role during the program implementation stage (Arnold 2021).

Taken together, this work has vastly expanded the potential universe of what policy process scholars consider "entrepreneurial" behavior. Moreover, the literature on policy entrepreneurship has, in some cases, evolved independent of the MSF. Indeed, many of the studies referenced above do not apply to the MSF. However, because policy entrepreneurship is so central to the MSF, the MSF research community is behooved to at least explore the extent to which existing MSF hypotheses need to be amended to better account for the existence of these new and novel types of entrepreneurs.

6.2 Methodological and Empirical Considerations

6.2.1 Empirically Test Existing Hypotheses with Greater Rigor

Despite important advancements in MSF research, empirical testing continues to lag behind. Many of the recent theoretical advancements have not been tested systematically, and a good part of the extant empirical research has either not taken the new theoretical insights into account or has not applied the MSF in a methodologically convincing way (or both). Hence, in the future, it will be very important for scholars to use the theoretical advancements and the methodological best practices we outline in this Element to improve MSF empirical research.

A number of scholars have put forward hypotheses, some of which we have presented in this Element. While the theoretical foundations have been laid, the empirical testing of the derived hypotheses has unfortunately not been forthcoming. What is needed for now is not necessarily more theory but more and better testing. As outlined in Section 1, studies on developing and autocratic countries are particularly welcome, as are studies on multilevel settings and international organizations. These and all other analyses need to engage in rigorous testing (see our point in Section 5) of the empirical implications of the MSF.

Qualitative research will particularly benefit from employing hypotheses as they help to make results comparable. Hence, using generic hypotheses will allow studies on different issue areas in different countries to speak to one another and help accumulate knowledge on the explanatory potential of the MSF. In many instances, it may be suitable to concentrate on one or a handful of hypotheses (e.g., only on one stream). Such a focus will facilitate a rigorous assessment of these hypotheses in depth through a single case. At the same time, it will also be important to test the overarching MSF hypothesis (Hypothesis 1) systematically, namely, that agenda change becomes more likely once all three streams are ready for coupling, a policy window opens, and a policy entrepreneur seeks to couple the streams. This is the core proposition of the framework, and hence a lot of effort should be put into assessing whether this expectation is correct.

At the same time, some caution is advisable when it comes to employing hypotheses in qualitative MSF studies. While hypotheses clearly help organize the analysis in a systematic way and help avoid storytelling, they also narrow down the focus on a few relations while many other aspects are disregarded. For example, while it is important to check whether proposals that fulfill the criteria for survival stand a better chance of getting coupled, as Hypothesis 4 in Section 2 would lead us to expect, it may also be important to analyze the whole softening-up process, depending on the research question – although this is not mirrored by one of the hypotheses. The point is to examine, although not necessarily in a single article, the broader policy processes within which individual elements are embedded to assess interaction or other effects or, at least, acknowledge the limitations of the study and continue the investigation in subsequent work. The same argument applies to other processes covered by the framework but not necessarily by the hypotheses. We gave some practical advice how to do this in Section 5. A circumscribed research question, clear definitions, and careful operationalization of concepts place fewer demands on data collection, increase transparency, and thus facilitate more rigorous testing.

MSF scholars should also take advantage of the potential that large-N studies may provide. While neither regression analyses nor QCA are without problems when it comes to testing the MSF, they clearly lend themselves to the analysis of some of the more particularistic hypotheses regarding the problem, politics, and policy streams. And while testing all elements of the theory in a single, comprehensive model may prove challenging, quantitative scholars can employ mixed methods designs to help explain those variables that may not lend themselves to modeling.

Whatever their preferred analytical strategy, it is imperative that MSF scholars remain vigilant in exploring and communicating new and novel ways to test the theory. It is our hope the strategies outlined in this Element as well as those described in Zohlnhöfer, Herweg, and Zahariadis' (2022) best practices chapter will help promote greater rigor in MSF research. However, many of these strategies are, above all else, suggestions that will require careful testing and refinement across time.

6.2.2 Continue Testing in Nondemocracies and Global Contexts

One of the most promising areas of MSF research has been the uptick in studies applying the framework to nondemocracies (Herweg, Zahariadis, and Zohlnhöfer 2022). Not only has this work been critical in exploring the generalizability of existing concepts in new governing contexts, but it has also generated new and exciting research directions. Van den Dool's (2023b) application of the theory to Chinese policymaking stands out as an exemplar study in terms of both its application and findings. Most importantly, van den Dool carefully adjusts the existing MSF hypotheses in order to better explain policymaking in authoritarian contexts, which, for obvious reasons, are quite different from democratic contexts. In doing so, she advances long-standing theoretical questions, which were largely born out of a desire to explain policymaking in Western democracies, while carving out space for appropriate theoretical adjustments in nondemocratic countries. Future research is behooved to, first and foremost, test her and Herweg, Zahariadis, and Zohlnhöfer's (2022) complementary hypotheses in other authoritarian contexts and, if needed, further adjusting hypotheses.

At the same time, global policymaking institutions, like the United Nations, World Health Organization, and scores of others, offer a fascinating context for assessing the MSF. The MSF seems particularly well suited for explaining policymaking in these contexts for two reasons. From climate change to pandemics, ambiguity is a hallmark of many of the issues global institutions are charged with managing, making the MSF an opportune theory for assessing their policy decisions. Second, because the MSF lends itself to both quantitative and qualitative applications, the theory will likely ease some of the methodological and data collection challenges that inevitably arise when studying global policy institutions. Indeed, the theory's analytical flexibility has already proven a boon for researchers studying nondemocratic contexts since it also allows them to develop fairly creative indicators of issue attention and agenda change – even in settings where accurate data is notoriously difficult to come by.

6.3 Conclusions

Nearly forty years since John Kingdon published *Agendas, Alternatives, and Public Policy* and the MSF has become one of the most prolific theories of agenda-setting and policy change. The last decade has marked a particularly important chapter in MSF's storied history as it has ushered in a new generation of scholarship grounded in a desire to develop shared hypotheses, to consistently apply and measure core concepts, and to rigorously test important policy research questions. This work has yielded exciting findings for not only MSF scholars but the larger policy community as well. Indeed, many of the concepts coined by Kingdon decades ago (e.g., focusing events and policy entrepreneurship) now constitute thriving sub-streams of research in their own right and have been readily integrated into other theories of policy change. Still, despite these important advances, more work is needed to continue to bolster the MSF's theoretical vitality, particularly through the systematic testing of core research questions and hypotheses.

References

Ackrill, Robert, and Adrian Kay. 2011. "Multiple Streams in EU Policymaking: The Case of the 2005 Sugar Reform." *Journal of European Public Policy* 18: 72–89.

Akgul, Arif, Halil Akbas and Ahmet Kule. 2019. "Probation System in Turkey: An Analysis of a Public Policy Formation Using Multiple Streams Framework." *International Journal of Comparative and Applied Criminal Justice* 43(4): 325–340.

Alvarez, Michael, Jose A. Cheibub, Fernando Limongi, and Adam Przeworski. 1996. "Classifying Political Regimes." *Studies in Comparative International Development* 31(2): 3–36.

Anderson, Sarah, Rob A. DeLeo, and Kristin Taylor. 2020. "Policy Entrepreneurs, Legislators, and Agenda Setting: Information and Influence." *Policy Studies Journal* 48(3): 587–611.

Anderson, William F., and David A. MacLean. 2015. "Public Forest Policy Development in New Brunswick, Canada: Multiple Streams Approach, Advocacy Coalition Framework, and the Role of Science." *Ecology and Society* 20(4): 20–32.

Arieli, Tamar, and Nissim Cohen. 2013. "Policy Entrepreneurs and Post-Conflict Cross-Border Cooperation: A Conceptual Framework and the Israeli-Jordanian Case." *Policy Sciences* 46(3): 237–256.

Arnold, Gwen. 2021. "Distinguishing the Street-Level Entrepreneurs." *Public Administration* 99(3): 439–453.

Asante, William. 2023. "The Multiple Streams Framework and Forest Policy Change Process in Ghana." *Politics and International Relations* 9(1): 1–13.

Babayan, Ararat, Caroline Schlaufer, and Arrtem Uldanov. 2021. "A Policy Window and a Network of Global and Local Policy Entrepreneurs: The Introduction of Opioid Substitution Therapy in Belarus." *Central European Journal of Public Policy* 15(2): 1–13.

Bache, Ian. 2013. "Measuring Quality of Life for Public Policy: An Idea Whose Time Has Come? Agenda-Setting Dynamics in the European Union." *Journal of European Public Policy* 20(1): 21–38.

Balla, Steven J. 2001. "Interstate Professional Associations and the Diffusion of Policy Innovations." *American Politics Research* 29(3): 221–245.

Bakir, Caner. 2009. "Policy Entrepreneurship and Institutional Change: Multilevel Governance of Central Banking Reform." *Governance* 22(4): 571–598.

Bandelow, Nils C., Colette S. Vogeler, Johanna Hornung, Johanna Kuhlmann, and Sebastian Heidrich. 2017. "Learning as a Necessary but Not Sufficient Condition for Major Health Policy Change: A Qualitative Comparative Analysis Combining ACF and MSF." *Journal of Comparative Policy Analysis: Research and Practice* 21(2): 167–182.

Baumgartner, Frank R., Christian Breunig, Christoffer Green-Pedersen, et al. 2009. "Punctuated Equilibrium in Comparative Perspective." *American Journal of Political Science* 53(3): 603–620.

Baumgartner, Frank R., Bryan D. Jones and Peter B. Mortensen. 2023. "Punctuated Equilibrium Theory: Explaining Stability and Change in Public Policymaking." In Christopher M. Weible, ed., *Theories of the Policy Process*. 5th ed., New York: Routledge.

Béland, Daniel, and Robert Henry Cox. 2016. "Ideas as Coalition Magnets: Coalition Building, Policy Entrepreneurs, and Power Relations." *Journal of European Public Policy* 23(3): 428–445.

Béland, Daniel, and Michael Howlett. 2016. "The Role and Impact of the Multiple-Streams Approach in Comparative Policy Analysis." *Journal of Comparative Policy Analysis: Research and Practice* 18(3): 221–227.

Bell, Michelle, Luis A. Cifuentes, Devra L. Davis, et al. 2011. "Environmental Health Indicators and a Case Study of Air Pollution in Latin American Cities." *Environmental Research* 111(1): 57–66.

Birkland, Thomas A. 1997. *After Disaster: Agenda Setting, Public Policy, and Focusing Events*. Washington, DC: Georgetown University Press.

Birkland, Thomas. 2004. "'The World Changed Today': Agenda-Setting and Policy Change in the Wake of the September 11 Terrorist Attacks." *Review of Policy Research* 21(2): 179–200.

Blum, Sonja. 2018. "The Multiple-Streams Framework and Knowledge Utilization: Argumentative Couplings of Problem, Policy, and Politics Issues." *European Policy Analysis* 4(1): 94–117.

Bolukbasi, H. Tolga, and Deniz Yıldırım. 2022. "Institutions in the Politics of Policy Change: Who Can Play, How They Play in Multiple Streams." *Journal of Public Policy* 42(3): 509–528.

Bossert, Thomas J., and Pablo Villalobos Dintrans. 2020. "Health Reform in the Midst of a Social and Political Crisis in Chile, 2019–2020." *Health Systems & Reform* 6(1): e1789031-1– e1789031-10.

Boswell, Christina, and Eugénia Rodrigues. 2016. "Policies, Politics, and Organizational Problems: Multiple Streams and the Implementation of Targets in UK Government." *Policy & Politics* 44(4): 507–524.

Box-Steffensmeier, Janet M., and Bradford S. Jones. 1997. "Time is of the Essence: Event History Models in Political Science." *American Journal of Political Science* 41(4): 1414–1461.

Brady, Henry E., and David Collier (eds.). 2010. *Rethinking Social Inquiry: Diverse Tools, Shared Standards.* 2nd expanded ed. Lanham, MD: Rowman & Littlefield.

Brunner, Steffen. 2008. "Understanding Policy Change: Multiple Streams and Emission Trading in Germany." *Global Environmental Change* 18(3): 501–507.

Budge, Ian, and Hans Keman. 1990. *Parties and Democracy: Coalition Formation and Government Functioning in Twenty States.* Oxford: Oxford University Press.

Bueno de Mesquita, Bruce, Alastair Smith, Randolph M. Siverson and James D. Morrow. 2003. *The Logic of Political Survival.* Cambridge, MA: MIT Press.

Bundgaard, Ulrik, and Karsten Vrangbæk. 2007. "Reform by Coincidence? Explaining the Policy Process of Structural Reform in Denmark." *Scandinavian Political Studies* 30(4): 491–520.

Cairney, Paul. 2018. "Three Habits of Successful Policy Entrepreneurs." *Policy and Politics* 46(2): 199–215.

Cairney, Paul, and Michael D. Jones. 2016. "Kingdon's Multiple Streams Approach: What is the Empirical Impact of this Universal Theory?" *Policy Studies Journal* 44(1): 37–58.

Capano, Giliberto, and Maria Tullia Galanti. 2021. "From Policy entrepreneurs to Policy Entrepreneurship: Actors and Actions in Public Policy Innovation." *Policy & Politics* 49(3): 321–342.

Carriedo, Angela, Karen Lock, and Benjamin Hawkins. 2020. "Policy Process and Non-State Actors' Influence On The 2014 Mexican Soda Tax." *Health Policy and Planning* 35(8): 941–952.

Carter, Neil, and Mike Childs. 2017. "Friends of the Earth as a Policy Entrepreneur: 'The Big Ask' Campaign for a UK Climate Change Act." *Environmental Politics* 27(6): 994–1013.

Carter, Ralph G., and James M. Scott. 2010. "Understanding Congressional Foreign Policy Innovators: Mapping Entrepreneurs and Their Strategies." *The Social Science Journal* 47(2): 418–438.

Ceccoli, Stephen, and Xinran Andy Chen. 2023. "Subnational Policy Windows: Shanghai's Grid Screening Policy." In Nikolaos Zahariadis, Nicole Herweg, Reimut Zohlnhöfer, and Evangelia Petridou, eds., *A Modern Guide to the Multiple Steams Framework.* Northampton, MA: Edward Elgar, pp. 265–284.

Cheibub, José Antonio, Jennifer Gandhi, and James Raymond Vreeland. 2010. Democracy and Dictatorship Revisited. *Public Choice* 143(1): 67–101

Cohen, Michael D., James G. March, and Johan P. Olsen. 1972. "A Garbage Can Model of Organizational Choice." *Administrative Science Quarterly* 17(1): 1–25.

Collier, David. 2011. "Understanding Process Tracing." *PS: Political Science & Politics* 44: 823–830.

Collier, David and James E. Mahon Jr. 1993. "Conceptual 'Stretching' Revisited: Adapting Categories in Comparative Analysis." *American Political Science Review* 87(4): 845–855.

Collins, Mary Elizabeth. 2018. "Comparative Analysis of State Policymaking in Child Welfare: Explaining Policy Choices." *Journal of Comparative Policy Analysis: Research and Practice* 20(4): 370–386.

Copeland, Paul, and Scott James. 2014. "Policy Windows, Ambiguity and Commission Entrepreneurship: Explaining the Relaunch of the European Union's Economic Agenda." *Journal of European Public Policy* 21: 1–19.

Cook, Jeffrey J., and Sara R. Rinfret. 2013. "The Environmental Protection Agency Regulates Greenhouse Gas Emissions: Is Anyone Paying Attentions?" *Review of Policy Research* 30(3): 263–280.

Craig, Rebekah L., Holly C. Felix, Jada F. Walker, and Martha Phillips. 2010. "Public Health Professionals as Policy Entrepreneurs: Arkansas's Childhood Obesity Policy Experience." *American Journal of Public Health* 100(11): 2047–2052.

Cummings, Amy, Katharine O. Strunk, and Craig De Voto. 2023. "'A Lot of States were Doing it': The Development of Michigan's Read by Grade Three Law." *Journal of Educational Change* 24: 107–132.

da Conceição, Hugo Rosa, Jan Börner, and Sven Wunder. 2015. "Why were Upscaled Incentive Programs for Forest Conservation Adopted? Comparing Policy Choices in Brazil, Ecuador, and Peru." *Ecosystem Services* 16: 243–252.

de Araújo, Fábio Resende, and Dinara Leslye Macedo e Silva Calazans. 2020. "Management of Food Security Actions during the COVID-19 Pandemic." *Brazilian Journal of Public Administration* 54(4): 1123–113.

DeLeo, Rob A. 2018. "Indicators, Agendas, and Streams: Analysing the Politics of Preparedness." *Policy & Politics* 46(1): 27–45.

DeLeo, Rob A. and Alex Duarte. 2022. "Does Data Drive Policymaking? A Multiple Streams Perspective on the Relationship Between Indicators and Agenda Setting." *Policy Studies Journal* 50(3): 701–724.

DeLeo, Rob A., Kristin Taylor, Deserai A. Crow, and Thomas Birkland. 2022. "During Disaster: Refining the Concept of Focusing Events to Better

Explain Long-Duration Crises." *International Review of Public Policy* 3(1): 5–28.

Derwort, Pim, Nicolas Jager, and Jens Newig. 2021. "How to Explain Major Policy Change Towards Sustainability? Bringing Together the Multiple Streams Framework and the Multilevel Perspective on Socio-Technical Transitions to Explore the German 'Energiewende'." *Policy Studies Journal* 50(3): 671–699.

Dolan, Dana A. 2021. "Multiple Partial Couplings in the Multiple Streams Framework: The Case of Extreme Weather and Climate Change Adaptation." *Policy Studies Journal* 49(1): 164–189.

Dolan, Dana A., and Sonja Blum. 2023. The Beating Heart of the MSF: Coupling as a Process. In Nikolaos Zahariadis, Nicole Herweg, Reimut Zohlnhöfer and Evangelia Petridou, eds., *A Modern Guide to the Multiple Streams Framework*. Cheltenham: Edward Elgar, 82–103.

Dolowitz, David P., and David Marsh. 2000. "Learning from Abroad: The Role of Policy Transfer in Contemporary Policy Making." *Governance* 13(1): 5–24.

Durant, Robert F., and Paul F. Diehl. 1989. "Agendas, Alternatives and Public Policy: Lessons from the U.S. Foreign Policy Arena." *Journal of Public Policy* 9(2): 179–205.

Eckersley, Peter, and Katarzyna Lakoma. 2021. "Straddling Multiple Streams: Focusing Events, Policy Entrepreneurs and Problem Brokers in the Governance of English Fire and Rescue Services." *Policy* Studies 43(5): 1001–1020.

Engl, Alice and Estelle Evrard. 2020. "Agenda-Setting Dynamics in the Post-2020 Cohesion Policy Reform: The Pathway towards the European Cross-Border Mechanism as Possible Policy Change." *Journal of European Integration* 42(7): 917–935.

Engler, Fabian and Nicole Herweg, 2019. "Of Barriers to Entry for Medium- and Large-n Multiple Streams Applications: Methodologic and Conceptual Considerations." *Policy Studies Journal* 47(4): 905–926.

Exworthy, Mark, and Martin Powell. 2004. "Big Windows and Little Windows: Implementation in the 'Congested State'." *Public Administration* 102(12): 2294–2302.

Faling, Marijn, and Robbert Biesbroek. 2019. "Cross-Boundary Policy Entrepreneurship for Climate-Smart Agriculture in Kenya." *Policy Sciences* 52: 525–547.

Fastenrath, Florian, and Paul Marx. 2023. "The role of Preference Formation and Perception in Unequal Representation. Combined Evidence from Elite Interviews and Focus Groups in Germany." Working Paper No. 26.

www.uni-due.de/imperia/md/content/soziooekonomie/ifsowp26_fastenrath marx2023.pdf (last accessed 17 October 2023).

Fischer, Sara, and Martin Strandberg-Larsen. 2016. "Power and Agenda-Setting in Tanzanian Health Policy: An Analysis of Stakeholder Perspectives." *International Journal of Health Policy and Management* 5(6): 355–363.

Fowler, Luke. 2019. "Problems, Politics, and Policy Streams in Policy Implementation." *Governance* 32(3): 403–420.

2022. "Using the Multiple Streams Framework to Connect Policy Adoption to Implementation." *Policy Studies Journal* 50(3): 615–639.

2023. *Democratic Policy Implementation in an Ambiguous World*. Albany: State University of New York Press.

Geddes, Barbara, Joseph Wright, and Erica Frantz. 2014. "Autocratic Breakdown and Regime Transitions: A New Data Set." *Perspectives on Politics* 12(2): 313–331.

Gerring, Jason. 2017. *Case Study Research*. 2nd ed. Cambridge: Cambridge University Press.

Geva-May, Iris. 2004. "Riding the Wave of Opportunity: Termination in Public Policy." *Journal of Public Administration Research and Theory* 14: 309–333.

Goyal, Nihit. 2022. "Policy Diffusion Through Multiple Streams: The (Non-) Adoption of Energy Conservation Building Code in India." *Policy Studies Journal* 50(3): 641–669.

Goyal, Nihit, Michael Howlett, and Namrata Chindarkar. 2020. "Who Coupled which Stream(s)? Policy Entrepreneurship and Innovation in the Energy-Water Nexus in Gujarat, India." *Public Administration and Development* 40(1): 49–64.

Green-Pedersen, Christoffer, and Peter B. Mortensen. 2010. "Who Sets the Agenda and Who Responds to it in the Danish Parliament? A New Model of Issue Competition and Agenda-Setting." *European Journal of Political Research* 49(2): 257–281.

Hahnkamper-Vandenbulcke, Nora. 2022. *Review Clauses in EU Legislation Adopted during the First Half of the Ninth Parliamentary Term (2019–2024): A Rolling Check-List*. Brussels: European Union, www.europarl.eur opa.eu/RegData/etudes/STUD/2022/734675/EPRS_STU(2022)734675_EN .pdf (last accessed 01 June 2023).

Harris, Mike, and Peter McCue. 2023. "Pop-Up Cycleways: How a COVID-19 'Policy Window' Changed the Relationship Between Urban Planning, Transport, and Health in Sydney, Australia." *Journal of the American Planning Association* 89(2): 240–252.

Hassanin, Ahmed, Serageldin Kamel, Imam Waked, and Meredith Fort. 2021. "Egypt's Ambitious Strategy to Eliminate Hepatitis C Virus: A Case Study." *Global Health: Science and Practice* 9(1): 187–200.

Heaphy, Janina. (2002). British counterterrorism, the international prohibition of torture, and the multiple streams framework." *Policy & Politics* 50(2): 225–241.

Herweg, Nicole. 2013. "Der Multiple-Streams-Ansatz – ein Ansatz, dessen Zeit gekommen ist?" *Zeitschrift für Vergleichende Politikwissenschaft* 7: 321–345.

2016. "Clarifying the Concept of Policy-Communities in the Multiple-Streams Framework." In Reimut Zohlnhöfer and Friedbert W. Rüb, eds., *Decision-Making under Ambiguity and Time Constraints: Assessing the Multiple-Streams Framework*. Colchester: ECPR Press, 125–145.

2017. *European Union Policy-Making: The Regulatory Shift in Natural Gas Market Policy*. Basingstoke: Palgrave Macmillan.

Herweg, Nicole, Christian Huß, and Reimut Zohlnhöfer. 2015. "Straightening the Three Streams: Theorizing Extensions of the Multiple Streams Framework." *European Journal of Political Research* 54(3): 435–449.

Herweg, Nicole, Nikolaos Zahariadis, and Reimut Zohlnhöfer. 2022. "Travelling Far and Wide? Applying the Multiple Streams Framework to Policy-Making in Autocracies." *Politische Vierteljahresschrift/German Political Science Quarterly* 63: 203–223.

Herweg, Nicole, Nikolaos Zahariadis, and Reimut Zohlnhöfer. 2023. "The Multiple Streams Framework: Foundations, Refinements and Empirical Applications." In Christopher M. Weible, ed., *Theories of the Policy Process*, 5th ed. New York: Routledge, 29–64.

Herweg, Nicole, and Nikolaos Zahariadis. 2018. "The Multiple Streams Approach." In Nikolaos Zahariadis and Laurie Buonanno eds., *The Routledge Handbook of European Public Policy*. New York: Routledge, 32–41.

Herweg, Nicole, and Reimut Zohlnhöfer. 2022. "Analyzing EU Policy Processes Applying the Multiple Streams Framework." In Paolo Graziano and Jale Tosun, eds., *Elgar Encyclopedia of European Union Public Policy*. Northampton, MA: Edward Elgar, 485–494.

Herweg, Nicole, and Reimut Zohlnhöfer. 2023. "Multiple Streams in Policy Implementation." In Fritz Sager, Celine Mavrot and Lael R. Keiser, eds., *Handbook of Public Policy Implementation*. Cheltenham: Edward Elgar.

Hoefer, Richard. 2022. "The Multiple Streams Framework: Understanding and Applying the Problems, Policies, and Politics Approach." *Journal of Policy Practice and Research* 3: 1–5.

Howlett, Michael. 2019. "Moving Policy Implementation Theory Forward." *Public Policy and Administration* 34(4): 405–430.

Howlett, Michael, Allan McConnell, and Anthony Perl. 2015. "Streams and Stages: Reconciling Kingdon and Policy Process Theory." *European Journal of Political Research* 54: 419–434.

Jakobsson, Elin. 2021. "How Climate-Induced Migration Entered the UN Policy Agenda in 2007–2010: A Multiple Streams Assessment." *Politics and Governance* 9(4): 16–26.

Johnstone, Rachael. 2018. "Explaining Abortion Policy Developments in New Brunswick and Prince Edward Island." *Journal of Canadian Studies* 52(3): 765–784.

Jones, Bryan D., Derek A. Epp, and Frank R. Baumgartner. 2019. "Democracy, Authoritarianism, and Policy Punctuations." *International Review of Public Policy* 1(1): 7–26.

Jones, Michael D., Holly L. Peterson, Jonathan J. Pierce, et al. 2016. "A River Runs Through It: A Multiple Streams Meta-Review." *Policy Studies Journal* 44(1): 13–36.

Kagan, Jennifer A. 2019. "Multiple Streams in Hawaii: How the Aloha State Adopted a 100% Renewable Portfolio Standard." *Review of Policy Research* 36(2): 217–241.

Kaunert, Christian, and Sarah Léonard. 2019. "The European Union's Response to the CBRN Terrorist Threat: A Multiple Streams Approach." *Politique Européenne* 65(3): 148–177.

Keeler, John T. S. 1993. "Opening the Window for Reform. Mandates, Crises, and Extraordinary Policymaking." *Comparative Political Studies* 25: 433–486.

Kingdon, John W. 2003[1984]. *Agendas, Alternatives, and Public Policies.* New York: Addison-Wesley Educational.

Koebele, Elizabeth. 2021. "When Multiple Streams Make a River: Analyzing Collaborative Policymaking Institutions using the Multiple Streams Framework." *Policy Sciences* 54: 609–628.

Knaggård, Åsa. 2015. "The Multiple Streams Framework and the Problem Broker." *European Journal of Political Research* 54 (3): 450–465.

Knaggård, Åsa, and Roger Hildingsson. 2023. "Multilevel Influence and Interaction in the MSF: A Conceptual Map." In Nikolaos Zahariadis, Nicole Herweg, Reimut Zohlnhöfer, and Evangelia Petridou eds., *A Modern Guide to the Multiple Streams Framework.* Cheltenham: Edward Elgar, 62–81.

Kristiansen, Elsa and Barrie Houlihan. 2015. "Developing Young Athletes: The Role of Private Sport schools in the Norwegian Sport System." *International Review of the Sociology of Sport* 52(4): 447–469.

Liu, Chun, and Krishna Jayakar. 2012. "The Evolution of Telecommunications Policy-Making: Comparative Analysis of China and India." *Telecommunications Policy* 36: 13–28.

Lovell, Heather. 2016. "The Role of International Policy Transfer within the Multiple Streams Approach: The Case of Smart Electricity Metering in Australia." *Public Administration* 94: 754–768.

Mintrom, Michael. 2019. *Policy Entrepreneurs and Dynamic Change.* Cambridge: Cambridge University Press.

Mintrom, Michael, and Phillipa Norman. 2009. "Policy Entrepreneurship and Policy Change." *Policy Studies Journal* 37(4): 649–667.

Möck, Malte, Colette Vogeler, Nils Bandelow, and Johanna Hornung. 2023. "Relational Coupling of Multiple Streams: The Case of COVID-19 Infections in German Abattoirs." *Policy Studies Journal* 51(2): 351–374.

Moghadam, Telma Zahirian, Pouran Raeissi, and Mehdi Jafari-Sirizi. 2019. "Analysis of the Health Sector Evolution Plan from the Perspective of Equity in Healthcare Financing: A Multiple Streams Model." *International Journal of Human Rights in Healthcare* 12(2): 124–137.

Mucciaroni, Gary. 2013. "The Garbage Can Model and the Study of the Policy-Making Process." In Eduardo Araral, Scott Fritzen, Michael Howlett, M. Ramesh, and Xun Wu, eds., *The Routledge Handbook of Public Policy.* New York: Routledge.

Münter, Michael. 2005. *Verfassungsreform im Einheitsstaat. Die Politik der Dezentralisierung in Großbritannien.* Wiesbaden: VS.

Nohrstedt, Daniel, Karin Ingold, Christopher M. Weible, et al. 2023. "The Advocacy Coalition Framework: Progress and Emerging Areas." In Christopher M. Weible, ed., *Theories of the Policy Process*, 5th ed. New York: Routledge.

Novotný, Vilém, Keiichi Satoh, and Melanie Nagel. 2021. "Refining the Multiple Stream's Framework's Integration Concept: Renewable Energy Policy and Ecological Modernization in Germany and Japan in Comparative Perspective." *Journal of Comparative Policy Analysis* 23(3): 291–309.

O'Donovan, Kristin. 2017. "An Assessment of Aggregate Focusing Events, Disaster Experience, and Policy Change." *Risk, Hazards & Crisis in Public Policy* 8(3): 201–219.

O'Neill, Brenda, Taruneek Kapoor, and Lindsay McLaren. 2019. "Politics, Science, and Termination: A Case Study of Water Fluoridation Policy in Calgary in 2011." *Review of Policy Research* 36(1): 99–120.

Pack, Simon M., and David P. Hedlund. 2020. "Inclusion of Electronic Sports in the Olympic Games for the Right (or Wrong) Reasons." *International Journal of Sport Policy and Politics* 12(3): 485–495.

Petridou, Evangelia, and Michael Mintrom. 2021. "A Research Agenda for the Study of Policy Entrepreneurs." *Policy Studies Journal* 49(4): 943–967.

Petridou, Evangelia, Roine Johansson, Kerstin Eriksson, Gertrud Alirani, and Nikolaos Zahariadis. 2023. "Theorizing Reactive Policy Entrepreneurship: A Case Study of Swedish Local Emergency Management." *Policy Studies Journal*, https://doi.org/10.1111/psj.12508.

Pierson, Paul. 2003. "Big, Slow-Moving, and ... Invisible: Macrosocial Processes in the Study of Comparative Politics." In James Mahoney and Dietrich Rueschemeyer, eds., *Comparative Historical Analysis in the Social Sciences*. Cambridge: Cambridge University Press, 177–207.

Potrafke, Niklas. 2017. "Partisan Politics: The Empirical Evidence from OECD Panel Studies." *Journal of Comparative Economics* 45(4): 712–750.

Rawat, Pragati, and John Charles Morris. 2016. "Kingdon's 'Streams' Model at Thirty: Still Relevant in the 21st Century?" *Politics & Policy* 44: 608–638.

Richardson, Jeremy. 1996. "Policymaking in the EU: Interests, Ideas and Garbage Cans of Primeval Soup." In Jeremy Richardson, ed., *European Union: Power and Policymaking*. London: Routledge, 3–30.

Ridde, Valéry. 2009. "Policy Implementation in an African State: An Extension of Kingdon's Multiple-Streams Approach." *Public Administration* 87(4): 938–954.

Rietig, Katharina. 2021. "Multilevel Reinforcing Dynamics: Global Climate Governance and European Renewable Energy Policy." *Public Administration* 99(1): 55–71.

Rietig, Katharina. 2023. "The Multiple Streams Framework and Multilevel Reinforcing Dynamics: The Case of European and International Climate Policy." In Nikolaos Zahariadis, Nicole Herweg, Reimut Zohlnhöfer and Evangelia Petridou, eds., *A Modern Guide to the Multiple Streams Framework*. Cheltenham: Edward Elgar, 285–304.

Roberts, Nancy C., and Paula J. King. 1991. "Policy Entrepreneurs: Their Activity Structure and Function in the Policy Process." *Journal of Public Administration Research and Theory* 1: 147–175.

Rüb, Friedbert W. 2014. "Multiple-Streams-Ansatz: Grundlagen, Probleme und Kritik." In Klaus Schubert and Nils C. Bandelow, eds., *Lehrbuch der Politikfeldanalyse*. München: Oldenbourg, 373–406.

Ryan, Daniel, and Marianna Micozzi. 2021. "The Politics of Climate Policy Innovation: The Case of the Argentine Carbon Tax." *Environmental Politics* 7: 1155–1173.

Sager, Fritz, Christian Rüefli, and Eva Thomann. 2019. "Fixing Federal Faults. Complementary Member State Policies in Swiss Health Care Policy." *International Review of Public Policy* 1(2): 147–172.

Sager, Fritz, and Eva Thomann. 2017. "Multiple Streams in Member State Implementation: Politics, Problem Construction and Policy Paths in Swiss Asylum Policy." *Journal of Public Policy* 37(3): 287–314.

Sanjurjo, Diego. 2020a. *Gun Control Policies in Latin America*. Cham: Palgrave.

2020b. "Taking the Multiple Streams Framework for a Walk in Latin America." *Policy Sciences* 53(1): 205–221.

2023. "More Guns, Less Violence? Putting the Multiple Streams Framework to the Test against Bolsonaro's Gun Liberalization Agenda." In Nikolaos Zahariadis, Nicole Herweg, Reimut Zohlnhöfer and Evangelia Petridou, eds., *A Modern Guide to the Multiple Streams Framework*. Cheltenham: Edward Elgar, 160–179.

Sartori, Giovanni. 1970. "Concept Misinformation in Comparative Politics." *The American Political Science Review* 64(4): 1033–1053.

Saurugger, Sabine, and Fabien Terpan. 2016. "Do Crises Lead to Policy Change? The Multiple Streams Framework and the European Union's Economic Governance Instruments." *Policy Sciences* 49: 33–53.

Schneider, Carsten Q., and Claudius Wagemann. 2012. *Set-Theoretic Methods for the Social Sciences: A Guide to Qualitative Comparative Analysis*. Cambridge: Cambridge University Press.

Schön-Quinlivan, Emmanuelle, and Marco Scipioni. 2017. "The Commission as Policy Entrepreneur in European Economic Governance: A Comparative Multiple Streams Analysis of the 2005 and 2011 Reform of the Stability and Growth Pact." *Journal of European Public Policy* 24(8): 1172–1190.

Schührer, Sabine. 2018. "Identifying Policy Entrepreneurs of Public Sector Accounting Agenda Setting in Australia." *Accounting, Auditing & Accountability Journal* 31(4): 1067–1097.

Schuler, Paul. 2020. "Position Taking or Position Ducking? A Theory of Public Debate in Single-Party Legislatures." *Comparative Political Studies* 53(9): 1493–1524.

Seawright, Jason, and John Gerring. 2008. "Case Selection Techniques in Case Study Research: A Menu of Qualitative and Quantitative Options." *Political Research Quarterly* 61(2): 294–308.

Sevenans, Julie. 2018. "One Concept, Many Interpretations: The Media's Causal Roles in Political Agenda-Setting Processes." *European Political Science Review* 10(2): 245–265.

Shephard, Daniel D., Anne Ellersiek, Johannes Meuer, et al. 2021. "Kingdon's Multiple Streams Approach in New Political Contexts: Consolidation, Configuration, and New Findings." *Governance* 34(2): 523–543.

Sieleunou, Isidore, Anne-Marie Turcotte-Tremblay, Jean-Claude Taptué Fotso, et al. 2017. "Setting Performance-Based Financing in the Health Sector Agenda: A Case Study in Cameroon." *Globalization and Health* 13(52): 2–15. https://doi.org/10.1186/s12992-017-0288-7.

Smith, Verna, and Jackie Cumming. 2017. "Implementing Pay-for-Performance in Primary Health Care: The role of Institutional Entrepreneurs." *Policy and Society* 36(4): 523–538.

Soroka, Stuart, and Christopher Wlezien. 2019. "Tracking the Coverage of Public Policy in Mass Media." *Policy Studies Journal* 47(2): 471–491.

Spohr, Florian. 2016. "Explaining Path Dependency and Deviation by Combing Multiple Streams Framework and Historical Institutionalism: A Comparative Analysis of German and Swedish Labor Market Policies." *Journal of Comparative Policy Analysis* 18: 257–272.

Spognardi, Andrés. 2020. "Cooperatives as a Buffer Between Capitalism's Conflicting Classes: The Pioneering Case of the Portuguese Cooperative Societies Act." *Journal of Policy History* 32(4): 439–462.

Ssengooba, Freddie, Aloysius Ssennyonjo, Timothy Musila, and Elizabeth Ekirapa-Kirachoa. 2021. "Momentum for Policy Change: Alternative Explanations for the Increased Interest in Results-Based Financing in Uganda." *Global Health Action* 14(1): 1948672. https://doi.org/10.1080/16549716.2021.1948672.

Staff, Helge. 2020. *The Political Economy of Private Security*. Wien/Zürich: Lit.

Tanaka, Yugo, Andrew Chapman, Tetsuo Tezuka, and Shigeki Sakurai. 2020. "Putting the Process into the Policy Mix: Simulating Policy Design for Energy and Electricity Transitions in Japan." *Energy Research and Social Science* 70: 463–473.

Taylor, Kristin, Stephanie Zarb, and Nathan Jeschke. 2021. "Ambiguity, Uncertainty and Implementation." *International Review of Public Policy* 3(1): 100–120.

Taylor, Kristin, Rob A. DeLeo, Stephanie Zarb, Nathan Jeschke, and Thomas A. Birkland. 2023. "Subnational Focusing Events and Agenda Change: The Case of Toxic Algae Bloom and Contaminated Drinking Water in Toledo, Ohio." In Nikolaos Zahariadis, Nicole Herweg, Reimut Zohlnhöfer, and Evangelia Petridou, eds., *A Modern Guide to the Multiple Steams Framework*. Northampton, MA: Edward Elgar, 222–245.

Tembo, Sydney and Seunghoo Lim. 2022. "Agenda Setting for the 20% Mandatory Subcontracting Policy in Zambia's Construction Sector:

The Multiple-Streams Framework." *Public Works Management & Policy* 28(2): 215–238.

Töller, Annette Elisabeth. 2023. "The Challenge of Applying the Multiple Streams Framework to Non-Decisions and Negative Decisions." In Nikolaos Zahariadis, Nicole Herweg, Reimut Zohlnhöfer, and Evangelia Petridou, eds. *A Modern Guide to the Multiple Steams Framework*. Northampton, MA: Edward Elgar, 305–326.

Tracy, Sarah J. 2019. Qualitative Research Methods: Collecting Evidence, Crafting Analysis, Communicating Impact 2nd Edition. Hoboken, New Jersey: Wiley-Blackwell.

Travis, Rick, and Nikolaos Zahariadis. 2002. "A Multiple Streams Model of U.S. Foreign Aid Policy." *Policy Studies Journal* 30(4): 495–514.

True, Jacqui, and Michael Mintrom. 2001. "Transnational Networks and Policy Diffusion: The Case of Gender Mainstreaming." *International Studies Quarterly* 45(1): 27–57.

Tsebelis, George, .2002. *Veto Players: How Political Institutions Work*. Princeton: Princeton University Press.

Turaga, Rama Mohana R., and Harsh Mittal. 2023. "The Policy Process of Adopting Environmental Standards for Coal Plants in India: Accommodating Transnational Politics in the Multiple Streams Framework." *Policy & Politics* 51(2): 334–361.

Tunstall, Ashley M., Christopher M. Weible, Elizabeth A. Tomsich, and Angela R. Gover. 2015. "Understanding Policy Reform in Colorado's Domestic Violence Offender Treatment Standards." *Social Policy & Administration* 50(5): 580–598.

Turnhout, Esther, Matthijs Hisschemöller, and Herman Eijsackers. 2007. "Ecological Indicators: Between the Two Fires of Science and Policy." *Ecological Indicators* 7: 215–228.

Van den Dool, Annemieke. 2023a. "The Multiple Streams Framework in an Autocracy: China's Long-Awaited Soil Pollution Law." In Nikolaos Zahariadis, Nicole Herweg, Reimut Zohlnhöfer and Evangelia Petridou, eds., *A Modern Guide to the Multiple Streams Framework*. Cheltenham: Edward Elgar, 200–221.

Van den Dool, Annemieke. 2023b. "The Multiple Streams Framework in a Nondemocracy: The Infeasibility of a National Ban on Live Poultry Sales in China." *Policy Studies Journal* 51(2): 327–349.

Venters, Monoka, Meghan V. Hauptli, and Lora Cohen-Vogel. 2012. "Federal Solutions to School Fiscal Crises: Lessons from Nixon's Failed National Sales Tax for Education." *Educational Policy* 26(1): 35–57.

Wahman, Michael, Jan Teorell, and Axel Hadenius. 2013. "Authoritarian Regime Types Revisited: Updated Data in Comparative Perspective." *Contemporary Politics* 19(1): 19–34.

Walgrave, Stefaan, Arno Jansen, Julie Sevenans, et al. 2023. "Inaccurate Politicians: Elected Representatives' Estimations of Public Opinion in Four Countries." *Journal of Politics* 85: 209–222.

Wang, Huihui, Adanna Chukwuma, Radu Comsa, et al. 2021. "Generating Political Priority for Primary Health Care Reform in Romania." *Health Systems & Reform* 7(2): e1898187-1–e1898187-10. https://doi.org/10 .1080/23288604.2021.1898187.

Weible, Christopher, and Samuel Workman, eds. 2022. *Methods of the Policy Process*. London: Routledge.

Wenzelburger, Georg, and Kathrin Hartmann. 2022. "Policy Formation, Termination and the Multiple Streams Framework: The Case of Introducing and Abolishing Automated University Admission in France." *Policy Studies* 43(5): 1075–1095.

Wenzelburger, Georg, and Stefanie Thurm. 2023. "Policy Termination Meets Multiple Streams, in: A Modern Guide to the Multiple Streams Framework." In Nikolaos Zahariadis, Nicole Herweg, Reimut Zohlnhöfer and Evangelia Petridou, eds., *A Modern Guide to the Multiple Streams Framework*. Cheltenham: Edward Elgar, 43–61.

Wolfe, Michelle, Bryan D. Jones, and Frank R. Baumgartner. 2013. "A Failure to Communicate: Agenda Setting in Media and Policy Studies." *Political Communication* 30(2): 175–192.

Wu, Yipin. 2020. "Dynamics of Policy Change in Authoritarian Countries: A Multiple-Case Study on China." *Journal of Public Policy* 40: 236–258.

Yin, Robert K. 2018. *Case Study Research and Applications: Design and Methods (6th ed.)*. Thousand Oaks, CA: Sage.

Zahariadis, Nikolaos. 1992. "To Sell or Not to Sell? Telecommunications Policy in Britain and France." *Journal of Public Policy* 12(4): 355–376.

1995. *Markets, States, and Public Policy: Privatization in Britain and France*. Ann Arbor: The University of Michigan Press.

1996. "Selling British Rail: An Idea Whose Time Has Come?" *Comparative Political Studies* 29(4): 400–422.

1999. "Ambiguity, Time, and Multiple Streams." In Paul Sabatier, ed., *Theories of the Policy Process*. Boulder, CO: Westview Press, 73–93.

2003. *Ambiguity & Choice in Public Policy: Political Decision making in Modern Democracies*. Washington, DC: Georgetown University Press.

2008. "Ambiguity and Choice in European Public Policy." *Journal of European Public Policy* 15(4): 514–530.

2013. "Leading Reform Amidst Transboundary Crises: Lessons from Greece." *Public Administration* 91(3): 648–662.

2015. "The Shield of Heracles: Multiple Streams and the Emotional Endowment Effect." *European Journal of Political Research* 54: 466–481.

2014. "Ambiguity and Multiple Streams." In Paul Sabatier, and Christopher M. Weible, eds., *Theories of the Policy Process*. Boulder, CO: Westview Press, 25–58.

Zahariadis, Nikolaos, and Christopher S. Allen. 1995. "Ideas, Networks, and Policy Streams: Privatization in Britain and Germany." *Policy Studies Review* 14(1/2): 71–98.

Zahariadis, Nikolaos, and Theofanis Exadaktylos. 2016. "Policies that Succeed and Programs that Fail: Ambiguity, Conflict, and Crisis in Greek Higher Education." *Policy Studies Journal* 44(1): 59–82.

Zahariadis, Nikolaos, and Evangelia Petridou. 2023. "Multiple Streams, Policy Implementation, and the Greek Refugee Crisis." In Nikolaos Zahariadis, Nicole Herweg, Reimut Zohlnhöfer and Evangelia Petridou, eds., *A Modern Guide to the Multiple Streams Framework*. Cheltenham: Edward Elgar, 144–160.

Zohlnhöfer, Reimut. 2009. "How Politics Matter When Policies Change: Understanding Policy Change as a Political Problem." *Journal of Comparative Policy Analysis* 11: 97–115.

2016. "Putting Together the Pieces of the Puzzle: Explaining German Labor Market Reforms with a Modified Multiple-Streams Approach." *Policy Studies Journal* 44: 83–107.

2023. "How Far does a Policy Change Go? Explaining the Scope of Reforms with the Multiple Streams Framework." In Nikolaos Zahariadis, Nicole Herweg, Reimut Zohlnhöfer and Evangelia Petridou, eds., *A Modern Guide to the Multiple Streams Framework*. Cheltenham: Edward Elgar, 25–42.

Zohlnhöfer, Reimut, Nicole Herweg, and Christian Huß. 2016. "Bringing Formal Political Institutions into the Multiple Streams Framework: An Analytical Proposal for Comparative Policy Analysis." *Journal of Comparative Policy Analysis* 18: 243–256.

Zohlnhöfer, Reimut, and Christian Huß. 2016. "How Well Does the Multiple-Streams Framework Travel? Evidence from German Case Studies." In Reimut Zohlnhöfer and Friedbert W. Rüb, eds., *Decision-Making under*

Ambiguity and Time Constraints: Assessing the Multiple-Streams Framework. Colchester: ECPR Press, 169–188.

Zohlnhöfer, Reimut, Nicole Herweg, and Nikolaos Zahariadis. 2022. "How to Conduct a Multiple Streams Study." In Christopher Weible and Samuel Workman, eds., *Methods of the Policy Process*. London: Routledge, 23–50.

Cambridge Elements ☰

Public Policy

M. Ramesh
National University of Singapore (NUS)

M. Ramesh is UNESCO Chair on Social Policy Design at the Lee Kuan Yew School of Public Policy, NUS. His research focuses on governance and social policy in East and Southeast Asia, in addition to public policy institutions and processes. He has published extensively in reputed international journals. He is Co-editor of *Policy and Society and Policy Design and Practice*.

Michael Howlett
Simon Fraser University, British Columbia

Michael Howlett is Burnaby Mountain Professor and Canada Research Chair (Tier 1) in the Department of Political Science, Simon Fraser University. He specialises in public policy analysis, and resource and environmental policy. He is currently editor-in-chief of *Policy Sciences* and co-editor of the *Journal of Comparative Policy Analysis, Policy and Society* and *Policy Design and Practice*.

Xun WU
Hong Kong University of Science and Technology

Xun WU is Professor and Head of the Division of Public Policy at the Hong Kong University of Science and Technology. He is a policy scientist whose research interests include policy innovations, water resource management and health policy reform. He has been involved extensively in consultancy and executive education, his work involving consultations for the World Bank and UNEP.

Judith Clifton
University of Cantabria

Judith Clifton is Professor of Economics at the University of Cantabria, Spain. She has published in leading policy journals and is editor-in-chief of the *Journal of Economic Policy Reform*. Most recently, her research enquires how emerging technologies can transform public administration, a forward-looking cutting-edge project which received €3.5 million funding from the Horizon2020 programme.

Eduardo Araral
National University of Singapore (NUS)

Eduardo Araral is widely published in various journals and books and has presented in forty conferences. He is currently Co-Director of the Institute of Water Policy at the Lee Kuan Yew School of Public Policy, NUS, and is a member of the editorial board of *Journal of Public Administration Research and Theory* and the board of the *Public Management Research Association*.

About the series

Elements in Public Policy is a concise and authoritative collection of assessments of the state of the art and future research directions in public policy research, as well as substantive new research on key topics. Edited by leading scholars in the field, the series is an ideal medium for reflecting on and advancing the understanding of critical issues in the public sphere. Collectively, it provides a forum for broad and diverse coverage of all major topics in the field while integrating different disciplinary and methodological approaches.

Cambridge Elements ☰

Public Policy

Elements in the Series

A full series listing is available at: www.cambridge.org/EPPO

Milton Keynes UK
Ingram Content Group UK Ltd.
UKHW030700120324
439302UK00017B/1171